FOCUSED
& FREE

Other Sound Wisdom Books
by John Martin

Empower Yourself: 7 Steps to Personal Success

Increase Your Personal Productivity: Your Guide to
Intentional Living & Doing More of What You Enjoy

Choose Your Perspective: 7 Tips for High Performance
through Intentional Thinking

FOCUSED & FREE

SIX STEPS FOR YOUR BUSINESS SUCCESS

JOHN MARTIN

Published and distributed by:

SOUND WISDOM
P.O. Box 310
Shippensburg, PA 17257-0310

717-530-2122

info@soundwisdom.com

www.soundwisdom.com

Cover/jacket designer: Eileen Rockwell

ISBN 13 TP: 978-1-64095-271-3

ISBN 13 eBook: 978-1-64095-272-0

For Worldwide Distribution, Printed in the U.S.A.

1 2 3 4 5 6 7 8 / 25 24 23 22 21

For D.G. Wild, thanks for the push.

*"Go confidently in the direction of your dreams.
Live the life you have imagined."*
—Henry David Thoreau

CONTENTS

INTRODUCTION

Whatever you're not changing, you're choosing.
—Laurie Buchanan, Author, Speaker

It's easy to say we have a goal, a dream, or a vision of success in our business or personal life—but what steps are we actually taking to accomplish that goal, dream, or vision?

I have discovered that when we narrow down our choices and goals into steps—the six steps discussed in this book—we can accomplish every goal, every dream, and make every vision come into vivid view, up close and personal.

Focusing on completing and repeating the necessary tasks in each step will bring out the best version of yourself in ways you never even imagined. Turning each of those steps into daily *good* habits will free us just as surely as some of our current *bad* habits imprison us, keeping us from moving forward in life.

"To achieve goals you've never achieved before, you need to start doing things you've never done before."
—Stephen Covey, Best-Selling Author

Think of the possibilities a disciplined set of steps that become habits can produce:

- Increased productivity at work or in your business
- More meaningful relationships at home
- A deeper understanding of yourself
- New ways to improve your lifestyle
- Enlarging your financial resources
- An infinite number of exciting opportunities waiting to be discovered

What could you accomplish if you distilled the constant and often useless, wavering thoughts into strict, emotionless actions that you automatically perform each morning and throughout the rest of the day—into focused and formidable thoughts and actions? This level of habitual action could totally change your life for the better.

Think about your daily life right now:

- What does it look like?

  - Chaotic? Unproductive? Boring?
  - Structured? Productive? Exciting?

- How do you start out each morning?

  - Grumpy and dreading the new day?
  - Happy to greet the new day?

- How consistent are you at accomplishing your daily, weekly, monthly tasks and/or goals?

  - Very consistent
  - Somewhat consistent
  - Not consistent

This book offers you six steps to take that will *free you* to alter your life in ways that will contribute positively to your business and personal success—*if* you are dedicated enough to follow through with your heart's desires and not fall victim to your momentary feelings or emotions.

Here is the challenge: Are you willing to make all six steps part of your daily routine so you can watch your business and your life improve in impressive ways you have never yet imagined?

If you are serious about being *Focused and Free,* these steps will become part of your lifestyle and will build your character into the person you knew you could be.

When you choose to make better choices on a daily basis, your focus will sharpen and your newfound freedom will lift you higher than your wildest dreams.

Success begins
in your imagination.

A SIX-STEP JUMP-START

1. Start by envisioning the person you wish to become and the successful business you hope to own. See in your mind and then write down on paper the details of how your business will look and operate, and what you will accomplish through its success.

> *"Create the highest, grandest vision possible for your life, because you become what you believe."*
>
> —Oprah Winfrey, Media Mogul

Imagine how you will spend your time. Then think about how you will act and feel as a person who successfully runs your own business. Picture this ideal and begin to believe your vision will come to fruition. Imagine as many details as possible—then write them down and make them come true using the steps presented in this book.

2. Organizing and planning are the next important steps to take. It's never too late nor too soon to start organizing your vision and planning for your success. The habit of planning is the beginning of focus. For example, Ray Kroc who was the founder of McDonalds didn't purchase his first burger and shake franchise until he was 52; Julia Child released her first cookbook at age 50; and Harland Sanders franchised KFC when he was 62. Whether or not you're in the food business, you can begin planning your success at any age in any endeavor.

Organizing your thoughts and ideas and then planning how to make your vision a reality takes you goal by goal through each day and through each step of growing your business and developing your character into the best version of yourself. Research, read, make lists, and seek advice during this stage—but be careful not to plan so much that you fail to take action.

3. Making daily progress defines part of what your improved focus and habits will help you to create. When you start seeing the results of your own work, you will desire to make more strides toward your goals on a daily, weekly, monthly, and yearly basis. Before you know it, you've embraced a lifelong habit of taking action and moving forward from the vision and organizing/planning phase into the operation and execution phase.

Remember the truism from statesman Frederick Douglass: "If there is no struggle, there is no progress."

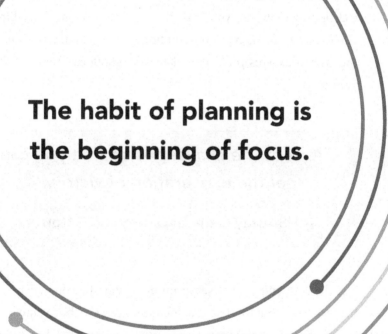

**The habit of planning is
the beginning of focus.**

4. *Making decisions quickly* might not come easily, especially if you're like me, a person by nature prone to overthinking and overanalyzing. But through conscious attempts, you can transform yourself into a business operator who arrives at decisions with a degree of urgency and sticks with them for as long as they prove to be correct. In short, you will become a decision-maker. *As a decision-maker, you will become confident.*

5. *Celebrate victories*—even if it seems to be a small achievement. Celebrating motivates you during times when you most need it and allows you to focus more on building up your confidence through the numerous wins you accumulate throughout each day. Celebrate your wins.

> "Accept the challenges so that you can feel the exhilaration of victory."
>
> —US Army General George S. Patton Jr.

6. *To keep going* takes self-training to stay the course when you least want to—but this habitual focus may prove to be the most valuable skill you pick up along your journey. As Winston Churchill said, "never give in, never give in, never, never, never—in nothing, great or small, large or petty—never give in except to convictions of honor and good sense." This hold true in business, relationships, and life in general.

When things are good and you are experiencing success, take advantage of the opportunities to grow so that you can continue with the work that has become your purpose in life.

And that's it.

If you develop and implement the following six steps described in full detail in the remainder of this book, you will build your character *and* your business into the vision you created within your mind.

It is a simple but focused formula that requires nothing more than the singleness of mind to stick with it and the time that is passing by each minute regardless of what you do.

Focus and free yourself
to become all
you want to be!

ENVISION YOUR GOAL

*"Dream and give yourself permission to
envision a you that you choose to be."*
—Joy Page, Casablanca Actress

Create a vision—it may start as a dream or daydream—that takes you to your goal. A vision does not remain a dream. A dream fades away after time, while a vision is something you can turn into a concrete reality. With a vision, you can create a roadmap, a blueprint to lay out the steps to achieve your goals.

ENVISION WHAT YOU WANT

I encourage you to take a few moments to really think about what you want in life.

Consider seriously the following questions and jot down the first thing that comes to mind. Then later, after reading this entire chapter, come back to these questions and write your thoughts:

- Do you imagine working for yourself and owning your own business?

- Do you envision being financially stable?

- Do you imagine more time to focus on your dreams?

- Do you envision a more fit, healthy body than what you see in the mirror today?

- Do you envision a loving relationship with a partner who supports your goals?

The focus is on business in this book, but relationships and physical health are definitely parts of the whole of you. Business, money, time, fitness, and love (whatever your definition) all meet at various points in life, and each are strong motivators.

MOTIVATE YOURSELF

Pay attention to your desires and formulate your vision. A clear vision increases your chance of success. Motivate yourself. No one can do it for you; and even on the occasion that someone does, you will quickly lose that motivation, so learn how to motivate yourself. Do whatever it takes to keep yourself constantly moving forward.

A clear vision increases
your chance of success.

Whether you want to get out of a bad job, relationship, housing situation, or lifestyle—or you want to strengthen circumstances that are already positive and promising, the keys are the same:

- Create your vision.
- Identify specifics.
- Write down the details.
- Speak it out loud.
- Go for it!

Envisioning your goal is the first step toward success in your business. It must be repeatable, applicable, and practical to almost any situation or goal you can imagine, so practice envisioning what you want in every aspect of your existence.

Napoleon Hill, hugely successful author of *Think and Grow Rich*, observed, "If you can conceive it, you can achieve it." That is a quote that is worthy of a post-it note on your mirror or a screenshot on your phone. It puts the onus on you to believe that what you can imagine, you can have.

And by the way, how quickly do you want to achieve your vision?

Patience is a virtue, yes. Patience is important in this journey to success. But in thinking about the big picture: *How long will you give yourself to achieve your goals?* Furthermore, what are you willing to give up to get there? Family gatherings, parties, sports? Netflix, YouTube, video games?

Are you willing to put up with friends and family gossiping about you because they don't understand what you're trying to do? Others may not understand why you rarely come around or don't want to hang out. They may not take the time to ask you what is going on in your life. They might talk about you behind your back, and you will have to live with that. Can you handle it?

Your business success comes with a price—personal sacrifice. Financial freedom and personal autonomy come only with significant investment in yourself. Long-term success is realized only when you understand the price and are willing to pay it; the rewards are worth the sacrifice.

Many successful people have concluded, *"Choose the pain of sacrifice over the pain of regret."*

Experiencing pain in life is part of being alive. The passing of time heals, but it also brings regret about the things we did not do. You can arrive at the end of life with fewer regrets by going all in now and using the time that you have to envision and build a life of success.

You can build a business that allows you the freedom and time to help others grow and to build relationships.

SELF-KNOWLEDGE

Are you the right person to build the business you want to build? Can you bring yourself through research and work to become the person you imagine yourself to be?

It is very important to be honest with yourself about who you are. For example, if you love food and wine, it's probably not realistic for

Be honest about who you are.

you to aim to be a professional bodybuilder or fitness model. But it may be realistic to have a cooking show on YouTube—and to exercise consistently to maintain good health.

Don't hold on to mistaken beliefs about yourself; they will only serve to limit your growth and achievement. Freely and honestly examine your life—likes, dislikes, habits, faith, routines, friends, beliefs, style, family, dreams, etc.

CREATING THE HABIT OF ENVISIONING GOALS

So how do you create the habit of envisioning goals? Make it real in your mind.

Some people recommend using the power of affirmative statements about your goal as if you've already achieved it. You can write those statements of affirmation on notecards and put them in various places in your apartment, house, workspace, and even your car.

Read them so often that the ideas begin to feel real. Examples:

- "I'm running a successful business and life is good."
- "I look forward to achieving my goals today!"
- "I take advantage of every opportunity."
- "I feel good about my appearance and look forward to my next workout."

- "The people in my life are important and there is mutual respect between us."

Positive affirmations about what you want to happen plants an image in your mind and makes each one real.

RESEARCH, READ, AND ABSORB SUCCESS STORIES

There are many audio products, books, and video content that not only tell the stories of business owners who are successful, but also explain the nuts and bolts of how to get there from where you are. The United States is full of people who have astonishing "rags to riches" life experiences that will encourage and motivate, and honestly, will leave you amazed at their determination to accomplish their vision.

I hope you will take the time to research many of these people who may and may not have familiar names, including but surely not limited to:

- John Paul DeJoria
- J.K. Rowling
- Do Won Chang
- Shania Twain
- Richard Branson
- Oprah Winfrey

- Shahid Khan
- Ralph Lauren
- Ursula Burns
- Jack Welch

While researching and reading about these people and others, pay particular attention to their focus, habits, lifestyles, and motivations. What can you learn from these real-life success stories?

Adopt the habit of observing and learning from others. Ask yourself:

- From among the stories, who do I admire most, and why?
- Who is living the lifestyle I would like to live?
- What can I do today to start making that happen?

Make a habit of reading, listening to, and watching the lives and techniques of others who have achieved what you want. It's all right there in front of you—on the screen of your phone and/or computer. You don't have to use your imagination except to interpret and translate how this information might work in your own life and business. Of course, it's always important to use credible sites and sources when researching on the Internet.

But still…

USE YOUR IMAGINATION!

> *"Lately, I have been wondering if there is time left for daydreaming in this 21st-century world of constant communication."*
>
> —James Thurber, Author of
> *The Secret Life of Walter Mitty*

Another way to practice this habit of envisioning is to allow your imagination to run wild. If you work a mindless job, for example, on an assembly line or a similar job that is more physical than mental, then take advantage of the lack of mental stress to begin creating something in your mind while on the job!

Or maybe you're at home relaxing on your recliner and your imagination runs to "What if" questions and you let yourself imagine in more detail. Think about what your ideal house would look like or what your ideal relationship would be like or how much money you would like to make through your business.

Many of us had the daydreaming taught out of us as children in school with, "Pay attention!" But it is an important part of forming a clear vision for what we want in our daily life, business, and long-term goals.

> *"The imagination has been called the scissors of the mind, and it is ever cutting, cutting, day by day, the pictures man sees there, and sooner or later, he meets his own creations in his outer world."*
>
> —Florence Scovel Shinn, Author of
> *The Game of Life and How to Play It*

Even if you are a fast-paced, non-stop type of person, work on carving out a little bit of time each day to be still and let your mind develop images of the life you want to live.

When you lay down to sleep at night, let yourself fall asleep to the visions of your future. This can be a perfect time to relax and imagine without fear or judgment.

In his famous novel *The Great Gatsby*, F. Scott Fitzgerald tells the story of a young man whose visions of love and grandeur consume him to the point where he works and angles his way up from living in poverty to hosting lavish parties attended by celebrities at his luxurious mansion off Long Island Sound in New York. In addition to Gatsby's love for a young lady, his work and actions were always driven by what he saw in his mind for his successful future. The following is an excerpt from the book that explains how important that is:

But his heart was in a constant, turbulent riot. The most grotesque and fantastic conceits haunted him in his bed at night. A universe of ineffable gaudiness spun itself out in his brain while the clock ticked on the washstand and the moon soaked with wet light his tangled clothes upon the floor. Each night he added to the pattern of his fancies until drowsiness closed down upon some vivid scene with an oblivious embrace. For a while these reveries provided an outlet for his imagination; they were a satisfactory hint of the *unreality of reality*, a promise that the rock of the world was founded securely on a fairy's wing.

There are so many possibilities and opportunities in the world, yet we place unnecessary limitations on our shoulders that prevent us from taking full advantage of what is at our doorstep. What if we stopped seeing the limitations and started seeing our imaginations? What if our daydreams became realities? What if we started dreaming real life scenarios? What a wild and wonderful world it would be!

VISION BOARDS

To make your goal crystal clear and to enforce it in your mind, think about it each morning and throughout the day. Know that one day your goal will become a reality. Whether your goal is business success, adhering to a fitness program, seeking financial freedom, or all three, using a vision board is a great way to keep that vision/goal in the forefront of your mind.

A vision board is simply posting pictures on a bulletin, mirror, or even the refrigerator things or people or places that represent your idealized goal. Make sure the board is placed where you will see it daily as a motivation tool and reminder of what your success will look like. Get creative—use different kinds of visuals that reveal the essence of your goal and vision.

In fact, you may want to have more than one board to reflect all of your goals. For instance, if your goal is to be the CEO of a home-building construction company, your photos may include undeveloped land nearby, construction sites, blueprints, homes in the price range you will be building, families who represent the happy home buyers, etc.

You may have another board that reflects the vision you have of being financially stable. That board may include a sample budget, a graph for savings, pages from a financial guru's book, articles from the *Wall Street Journal,* etc.

And if you are seeking a fit body and healthy lifestyle, your vision board would probably include magazine photos of people who epitomize the shape you want, a suitable diet complete with recipes, an exercise plan and schedule, people biking or hiking, a list of dos and don'ts, etc.

Pictures create emotions, which you can use to focus on creating action. Tangibles create a more solid vision—something you can grasp onto physically as well as mentally.

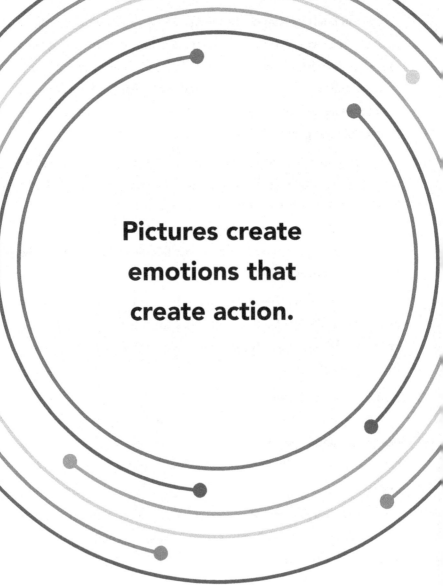

Pictures create
emotions that
create action.

JOURNALING

Journaling is another great way to clarify your vision and solidify the details of your vision in your mind. When you write down your thoughts each day, you can free yourself to be honest and open with exactly what it is you're seeking. I encourage you to write anything and everything as it comes to mind about each goal and each step you are going to take to get there.

Knowing you are the only person who will read your journal, you can write your most pure and honest thoughts—and from these thoughts, you can learn all kinds of useful information about the way you think and what your strengths and weaknesses are. This is valuable information to use in your business as well as in your personal life.

HAVE A GOOD DAY AT WORK

Start envisioning a better way, a better view of life—beginning right where you are. For example, practice envisioning (and accomplishing) goals even if you work at a job you don't like. Dream up different techniques to envision a good day every day at work.

Maybe a good day is being busy and productive so your coworkers (and boss) see you as a conscientious and dependable person. Or maybe a good day is completing your least favorite task first thing in the morning so the rest of the day is smooth sailing. Whatever it is, envision the work being done and your day being productive, even when you see no other positive elements to the job.

When you see yourself as successful even in negative situations, you will put yourself in a positive mental attitude!

As you continue to imagine your big-picture vision as well as work on envisioning your long-term goals while accomplishing the daily ones, you will notice a strength of resolve beginning to form within you. This is confidence. And it will grow and grow until you believe with your whole being that you *will* accomplish what you've set out to accomplish. It becomes so real in your mind through envisioning that it almost seems easy.

Of course, it takes effort to form habits of this type, but it is well worth the time and determination to visualize what you are working on becoming.

The habit of envisioning your own success starts as an exercise of the mind, but ends up being the engine that fuels your physical action toward reaching your goals. When the habit is repeated over the course of reaching many smaller goals, then onto bigger goals, you are on your way to achieving the success and independence you want in your business and life.

To build the habit of envisioning your success:

- Let your mind wander in any and all directions.
- Imagine the specifics and fill in the details.
- Create a clear vision.
- Write down each vision.

Self-reflection is a critical part of getting started and growing beyond your current status.

A strength of resolve
will form—and
confidence will grow.

- Do the actual work to bring the vision to life.
- Always be aware of and pay attention to your thoughts; allow them to drift into fantasy that can become future visions.

We don't have to be too hard on ourselves, too strictly regimented that we're constantly concentrating on being "present" every single moment—sometimes being present is intentionally imagining a future.

To create a new good habit, do this over and over again as often as you can: Imagine yourself as the successful business owner you desire to be. Imagine yourself physically fit, in the best shape of your life no matter your current age or circumstances. Imagine the family you desire to be part of and the house in which you all will live.

This habit leads to the doing that leads to the being. Change your belief system by imagining something so real, detailed, and frequent in your mind that it is natural to begin seeing this vision in your life. The line between imagination and real life will blur, and you will slip into that beautiful future you imagined, sooner than later.

> *"We need only in cold blood act as if the thing in question were real, and keep acting as if it were real, and it will infallibly end by growing into such a connection with our life that it will become real."*
>
> —William James, American Philosopher

PROTECT YOUR VISION

Be careful with whom you share your goals and vision for your life. There are people who will (maybe not intentionally) discourage you due to their own insecurity or jealousy. Only talk about your goals to those you know will encourage, motivate, or give you wise advice. Talk to those who are practicing similar habits for success in their lives when it comes to setting and reaching goals.

On the other hand, it can be helpful to share your vision if you are motivated by the doubt and criticism of others, or if you need to create some accountability by putting your goals out there. This is a personal choice and it depends on how you work best; but when you are just beginning to develop your habits for success, you may not want too much external pressure—or unnecessary opinions.

RELEASE ANXIETY

It's true that the actual doing and achieving is what builds confidence and weakens self-doubt. It is also true that creating and maintaining a clear vision of your goal lessens the damaging effects of anxiety. Anxiety about failure can be crippling. Anxiety about success can be stagnating.

The anxiety of not knowing what success looks like or what is supposed to be done causes many people to become trapped where they are in life.

**Sometimes
being present is
intentionally imagining
a fruitful future.**

Free yourself
to imagine.

And the anxiety of succeeding and not being prepared for it is a more common problem than we want to admit as well.

Maybe the worry comes from the fear of change. After all, success means you have to leave your comfort zone to realize it.

How can you let go of who you think you are to free yourself to be someone different?

After you clarify your vision in your mind, work out the details, and have the habit of envisioning success via mental awareness, working toward triumph is less ominous, vague, and overwhelming. It becomes, again, much closer to reality than a dream. Just like the monster you imagine is usually worse than the one you would ever see, so it is with the obstacles between you and your goals.

CONFIDENCE, NOT FEAR

Our goals start out almost dreamlike, far away, and unrealistic until we put in the mental work to create something out of the vague, shadowy shapes in our mind's eye, something distinct. We must imagine over and over again until the goal becomes a scenario we are on the verge of and are ready to live. Then we realize that some elements of our imagined, dreamed, and fantasized future are already parts of our reality!

What is there to be afraid of? It's already happening!

There's no real need to fear the sales pitch when you've already seen yourself succeed in selling it so many times before. And of course, each actual pitch and sell (goal and achievement) goes a long way toward building your confidence.

Your success begins with your habit of envisioning a future that changes your internal belief system. Eventually, you stop repeating the negative things you used to say to yourself. There is a sense of acceptance that you have achieved through the vision. You have let the old self die and fall away—and have welcomed the new and improved self, ready to take on every opportunity!

The idea is to seek a vision that gives you purpose in life and then to implement that vision. The vision by itself is one half, one part, of a process. It implies the necessity of living that vision, otherwise the vision will sink back into itself.

—Lewis P. Johnson

PEN TO PAPER

Write down in one sentence a goal you have for yourself, the YOU you want to be:

_____

_____

_____

_____

Now write down specific details about this vision—as many as you can think of and really let yourself make it as big and grand as you want. (You may want to keep this in a notebook, on a note card, or in your phone/tablet for reviewing later.)

_____

_____

_____

_____

_____

_____

_____

In a couple weeks, do the same exercise and compare your notes. You are creating the initial blueprint—the reality—of what is to come.

> *"Good business leaders create a vision, articulate the vision, passionately own the vision, and relentlessly drive it to completion."*
>
> —Jack Welch, former General Electric CEO

THE $10 MILLION CHECK

Famous actor Jim Carrey often tells the story of how, many years before he was making a living through his acting, he wrote a check out to himself in the amount of $10 million. He put in the note line: *for acting services rendered.* He carried this check in his wallet as he worked restaurant jobs and other odd jobs to get by while he auditioned and continued working toward his goal of being a full-time actor.

Ten years later, after the check he carried was tattered and torn from the years in his wallet, Carry was given a legitimate check for $10 million for an acting job. His story is a perfect example of how envisioning your goal down to the smallest detail can be helpful in bringing your dreams to fruition. By the way, Carrey's estimated net worth as of this writing is $180 million.

ALL THE SMALL THINGS

You may not consider all of your goals big or significant accomplishments, but establishing a habit of accomplishing small goals becomes a habit of accomplishing big goals. For example, going to the hardware store to buy items to complete a necessary home repair may not seem like a big deal, but when you look at that finished repair project, your sense of satisfaction comes from completing all the small goals on your to-do list—which forms a powerful habit!

Pay attention to the little wishes you have. Examples may include:

- Getting up earlier in the morning to exercise.
- Cleaning your house more often.
- Relaxing more with friends.
- Preparing healthier meals.
- Reading more about your business interests.

All these goals can be achieved through the same six-step program for forming successful habits you are reading about here. The whole idea behind forming habits is to build a successful mentality through training your mind to envision goals, plan, execute, persevere, and then celebrate even down to the smallest imaginable goal.

In fact, *start* with the smallest goal. The starting point to developing the habit of envisioning your goals is to break it down to the smallest one. For instance:

A habit of
accomplishing small
goals becomes a habit
of accomplishing
big goals.

- What does the meal look like that you envision eating tonight?
- How will you feel after preparing and eating that deliciously healthy meal?
- How does it feel eating that meal in your freshly cleaned kitchen?
- After dinner, how much more confident do you feel after reading about the current trends in your business?
- How much healthier and happier will you be after getting up early and jogging with friends, then enjoying a smoothie together afterward?

Envisioning the smallest goals begins the habit. When you habitually envision your future no matter how immediate, you are building the foundation to accomplish your bigger goals and dreams through this habit.

POSITIVE SELF-TALK

Positive self-talk is the only way to keep from falling into the trap of negativity, which always leads to defeat.

Reject:

- A poverty mindset
- The attitude that "This is just the way life is."
- The idea of quitting
- Feelings of lack and misery

Accept:

- A positive mindset
- The attitude that "I envision success!"
- The vision that will become my reality
- Habits of gratitude, achievement, and triumph

Remember, the key is to develop good habits through the seemingly mundane details of your life, which are vital when transitioning into a different, more exciting and fulfilling way of living.

Keep your mind on the great and splendid thing you would like to do; and then, as the days go gliding by, you will find yourself unconsciously seizing the opportunities that are required for the fulfillment of your desire, just as the coral insect takes from the running tide the elements that it needs. Picture in your mind the able, earnest, useful person you desire to be, and the thought that you hold is hourly transforming you into that particular individual you so admire.

**—Elbert Hubbard,
Publisher and Philosopher**

QUESTIONS TO CONSIDER

- What do you envision as an ideal life? Describe it in detail.
- Do you notice any common threads or themes in your daydreaming or imagined ideals? Write them down and compare them.
- How much money would the "ideal you" earn per year? Where would you live?
- How many hours per week do you envision yourself working in the most ideal situation you can imagine?
- Would you spend more time with your family?
- How much money would you have in your savings and checking accounts?
- Would you work from home?
- Would you travel?
- Would you have the courage to speak in public or talk to strangers freely in your ideal scenario?
- Are you willing to do whatever it takes to find success in your ideal career?

Step 2

ORGANIZE AND PLAN

"If you talk about it, it's a dream; if you envision it, it's possible; but if you schedule it, it's real."
—Tony Robbins, Author and Speaker

The next step is to organize and plan—taking your dream and envisioning it and then organizing the details and planning to make it real. This step frees you from the emptiness of broken dreams and forgotten lives you wish you had lived.

The majority of this chapter is working on habits that develop the right focus; a strong, positive mental state that allows you to form routines, organize, and schedule your dreams into reality.

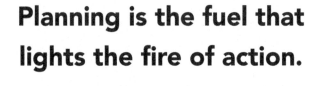

Planning is the fuel that lights the fire of action.

ORGANIZE

Unlike organizing a file cabinet full of paperwork, you must organize your thoughts, dreams, visions, and ideas before you can actually make any progress. Psychologists have discovered that humans have more than 6,000 thoughts per day.[1]

RESEARCH SUCCESS IN YOUR INDUSTRY

Again, I encourage you to research and read, watch videos and podcasts, and listen to audio books of *success stories* that apply to your specific field of interest. In every area of endeavor, there are people who have excelled—and you can learn so much from their trials and errors...and ultimate success.

In doing this research, you are following others who have done so and who learned more than enough to make them famous, rich, and even legendary. For instance, Napoleon Hill researched and interviewed hundreds of wealthy and successful people—including Andrew Carnegie and Charles M. Schwab—and from the wisdom gleaned from those encounters, he wrote the wildly popular book, *Think and Grow Rich.*[2] Zig Ziglar is known to have influenced more than a billion people through his books on personal achievement in which he shares hundreds of tactics to make dreams come true.[3]

And Jim Stovall—entrepreneur, author, movie producer—researched and reached out to Ted Turner when he envisioned the Narrative Television Network, a totally unique concept of making the visual world accessible for blind people, which became a very successful company that has touched millions of lives worldwide. He also researched and reached out to Steve Forbes when organizing and planning to expand his business within the financial realm.[4]

To find out as many details as possible about how people in your field became successful, it may be helpful to create a list of important questions you want to find answers to when researching. For just a few examples, you may want to discover the answers to how your subjects:

- Developed their vision
- Organized their thoughts and ideas
- Came up with a game plan
- Implemented the plan
- Funded the project
- Handled setbacks
- Handled success

Find out as many details as you can find about how they got from where they were to where they wanted to be—so you can mimic or adjust your plan to get from where you are to where you want to be. As closely as possible, describe in words or symbols or images these ideas.

Just like you would refer to a map or your GPS navigation system before going to a location you've never been before, I encourage you to explore all the materials available that provides information about the people who have earned success personally or professionally.

There is so much information on the Internet and in books that you can design your own style of learning or reading with the click of your computer mouse or phone keyboard.

I recommend reading only credible sources—not gossip tabloids, biased authors, commercialized chatter—that provide information about people who have accomplished what you would like to accomplish. Add to the previous list of questions:

- What did they do to get where they are?
- How did they start?
- What motivates them to keep going?
- Why did they choose their particular career?
- What key skills have they acquired?
- What are their daily habits?

It is very important to keep meticulous notes or comments in the margins so you can refer to them when you need inspiration or a jump-start on a dreary day.

HABIT-FORMING HABITS

It is important to develop the skill of concentration and follow-through. Start with a daily to-do list that you absolutely know would be good for you to do each day. You may want to begin with only one or two things, but the key is to start—which will become a habit that will move you closer and closer to achieving your goal.

What is on your list are not New Year's Resolutions that are just good intentions that quickly disappear with a turn of the calendar page. These are potentially life-changing steps to a focused and free life you've been dreaming about and are ready to bring to reality.

Your list may begin with any or all of the following:

- Write for 15 minutes in my journal.
- Take a 20-minute walk.
- Read a current business-related article for 30 minutes.
- Read a novel for 30 minutes every day.
- Greet everyone you see today with a smile.
- Give at least one person a sincere compliment.
- Think of ten things you are thankful for.
- Watch an educational television show.
- Watch a sitcom.
- Enjoy the sunrise and/or the sunset.
- Praise your spouse, children, and yourself for jobs well done.

As mentioned previously, establishing small habits leads to bigger, more significant habits that will carry you forward toward turning your vision into your reality.

GET PAID TO LEARN

Working in the industry that you may want to start your own independent business is a great way to get your feet wet. Dive in and find a job in the field of your choice. Learn everything you can about the business, the products, and the operating processes. Watch the top performers and try to find a mentor among them so you can ask questions and learn even more.

Many times we are in such a hurry to do our own thing that we miss a fantastic opportunity to lessen our future mistakes by taking the time to learn from people and businesses that have been doing for years what we want to begin.

FROM THE BOTTOM UP

You might find the following very interesting; portions taken from an article on *YoungUpStarts.com* titled "From Mailroom to Boardroom: 10 Modern-Day Execs Who Started at the Bottom":

> *George Bodenheimer* got in on ESPN in the network's infancy, starting just 16 months after the launch. His first jobs? Bodenheimer worked in the mailroom and also in the administrative department. He worked his way up through the company; and after 17 years, he earned the position of Executive Chairman of ESPN Inc. in 2012.

David Geffen was a three-time college dropout working in the mailroom at William Morris Agency. Now he's known for his multiple record labels and his part in founding DreamWorks, a major film studio with partners Steven Spielberg and Jeffery Katzenberg.

Jim Skinner worked as a restaurant manager trainee. From that early management position, Skinner worked his way up through the ranks. In 2004, Skinner was named CEO of McDonald's Corp and under his leadership the company increased sales by almost $20 billion.[5]

And then there is the founder of Spanx, Sara Blakely, a billionaire who started her empire at age 27 with only $5,000 of personal savings. She was a selling fax machines door to door when she came up with the idea—the vision—for Spanx, women's slimming undergarments. Her milestones along the way:

1998: Sara Blakely starts SPANX while selling fax machines with $5,000 in savings.

1999: Spanx's first year revenue tops $4,000,000.

1999: Blakely's product distributed into Neiman Marcus.

2000: Oprah names SPANX her favorite product of the year and sales hit $10,000,000 in revenue.

2001: SPANX is featured on QVC and sells more than 8,000 units in less than six minutes.

2012: Blakely named the world's youngest, self-made female billionaire by *Forbes Magazine* and one of *TIME's* 100 Most Influential People.[6]

A few of Blakely's quotes worth contemplating:

"You have to visualize where you're headed and be very clear about it. Take a polaroid picture of where you're going to be in a few years."

"My dad encouraged us to fail. Growing up, he would ask us what we failed at that week. If we didn't have something, he would be disappointed. It changed my mindset at an early age that failure is not the outcome, failure is not trying. Don't be afraid to fail."

"Don't be intimidated by what you don't know. That can be your greatest strength and ensure that you do things differently from everyone else."

"It's important to be willing to make mistakes. The worst thing that can happen is you become memorable."

"Don't solicit feedback on your product, idea or your business just for validation purposes. You want to tell the people who can help move your idea forward; but if you're just looking to your friend, co-worker, husband or wife for validation, be careful. It can stop a lot of multimillion-dollar ideas in their tracks in the beginning."[7]

> *"Don't be afraid to take time to learn.*
> *It's good to work for other people. I*
> *worked for others for 20 years.*
> *They paid me to learn."*
>
> —Vera Wang, Fashion Designer

MONEY MATTERS

Another benefit of starting with a job is that it allows you to accumulate startup capital for your independent business. During this step of organizing and planning, you need to determine how much money will you need. Research and even a trip to a financial accountant or trusted friend with financial acumen may be necessary. Keep a record of your findings in your journal or business planning notebook. Come up with a target amount and make it your goal to save that much.

Develop the habit of saving and being frugal in order to accomplish your goals. When you have a specific amount written down, find a way to keep that number in front of you or in your mind prominently as motivation.

When making purchases, first ask yourself:

- Do I really need to stop for an expensive cup of coffee when I can make it at home for a lot less?

- Is a new car necessary or would a good, pre-owned car with few miles be a better choice?

- Do I need another pair of shoes, really?

There are all kinds of ways to save money, and if we have a reason to do it, we are more likely to be alert and aware of when we are spending money unnecessarily. And definitely avoid the trap of paying for things with a credit card. Paying exorbitant interest rates is not worth whatever it is you could save and pay for up-front. Credit card debt is financial bondage! Remember, you are seeking financial *freedom.*

FREEDOM THROUGH FINANCE

To be *free financially,* take to heart these proven-successful principles of frugal living:

- Save money.

- Avoid debt.

- Invest your savings.

- Do not spend more than you earn.

In his book *The Richest Man in Babylon*, George Clason outlines principles to follow in order to become wealthy. In our case, if we follow these principles we can become free of financial stress.

Some principles included in this classic book:

- Pay yourself first. Put aside 10 percent of everything you earn. Do this before you pay your bills, buy your food, or spend money on anything else.

- Do not put all your eggs in one basket. When you invest, make sure you invest your money in different means of returns— real estate, various stocks, precious metals, cash, etc.

- Spend in moderation. Even if you are making a lot of money, do not overspend for the sake of it. Practice restraint in spending just as you would in other areas of your life.

- Look for ways to continue to be able to earn money as you grow older.

I encourage you to read this book and follow the principles and instructions—and you will find yourself on the path to financial independence. Invest in yourself. In addition to this book, there are many resources available to take you step by step through the process of becoming debt free, saving money in various ways, investing money to earn more money, and finding ways to increase your earning power.

EXERCISE

When you are organizing and planning for your physical well-being, I encourage you to make it a goal, a habit, to exercise in the morning for at least 15 minutes. Try to make it happen every day— no matter what.

When you are in your planning phase of your goals, you need to have a clear head, a clean conscience, and a body full of energy, not fatigue.

Whether it's a walk, a run, a swim, calisthenics workout, lifting weights, or a combination of these things, any type of movement to get your heart rate up and your body moving in the morning will go a long way to helping you engage a positive mental attitude to start the day.

Every time I go long periods of time without exercising, my body eventually begins to ache and cry out for relief. Even so, I feel overwhelmed thinking about going to the gym. The weights seem like they weigh a ton. Discouragement and procrastination ensue and my physical and mental wellness decline.

But when I gain control of my attitude—the key for me to get back into the exercise routine has always been to take a walk—I feel much better overall. I am a more positive person after taking a 15-minute walk every day.

Taking a walk is simple but so very healthy for body, mind, and spirit. It can be just what you need to jumpstart yourself into a healthier daily routine.

TO-DO LIST IN THE MORNING

Start your morning by writing down your goals for that day. Organizing your day's goals could include nonbusiness related tasks such as getting groceries or cleaning your living space because these types of seemingly unrelated activities do affect work on your business.

The point of your to-do list in the morning is to get the ideas of what you want to accomplish out of your head and onto the paper, or screen, in front of you. This way you can see it, organize and prioritize your action items—then feel the satisfaction of crossing them off the list after you complete each task. Keep the list on your person so you can remember to work on completing each task that day.

STAY ON SCHEDULE

Place value on others' time and your own. You can do this by keeping a schedule and sticking to the time allotted for meetings, phone calls, and other scheduled tasks as much as possible. A day planner is a perfect tool for this effort. Schedule your phone calls and appointments throughout the day ahead of time down to the half hour or hour, if possible. Being organized and planning ahead preserves mental space for creative thinking.

Punctuality counts! Make it a habit to always call when you say you will and show up for appointments when you say you will. Not only does this show the other person or people that you respect their time, it also develops a mutual-respect relationship. Adhering to your schedule allows you to manage your time, which in the long run alleviates the stress of feeling rushed or being impolite.

EVALUATE THE DAY

I look forward to evaluating the day's accomplishments before going to bed at night. I have adopted the habit of reviewing my morning to-do list and seeing the tasks that were completed throughout the day. Then I take time to think about and recognize the progress I made plus the tasks that remain and need to be added to the next day's to-do list.

You may want to start this process as well. Consider using this time in the evening to begin the next day's to-do list—that way you are already putting motivating, action-minded thoughts into your head before lying down to sleep.

You may also want to organize your plans for the next day—meal prep, child care, working ahead, etc.—which will give you a head start and give your mind time to rest and enjoy a good night's sleep.

Allow time for reflection, prayer, and/or meditation each day. Typically I like to do this in the morning and evening for at least 15 minutes at a time. Do what works for you, but it's important to have periods of non-activity when you allow yourself to unwind and relax. Time spent like this can invite mental breakthroughs in areas where you might be having a hard time seeing what the next step is and in which direction you should go.

SELF-REFLECTION QUESTIONS

During your downtimes, you may want to ask yourself questions such as:

- What did I get done today?
- When did I surprise myself by what I accomplished today?
- Did I overcome any obstacles?
- What uncomfortable situations did I succeed in navigating?
- How can I plan to free up more time tomorrow?
- What kind of person do I admire enough to want to be?
- During my childhood years, what was I drawn to and interested in?
- What would I rather be doing to earn money?
- Would I rather live a more minimalistic and simple life? Or a fast-paced, more adventurous one? A mixture of both?
- Am I cynical about the world I was born into?
- How can I improve my world, my relationships?

Answering honestly these and similar types of questions will give you the answers you are *really* seeking when you look outward and chase pleasure or try to escape from the pain of your existence through vices.

We are meant to live honest lives and be content. Don't short-change yourself by seeking only money and the trappings of what you believe is expected of you to fulfill the "American dream" or someone else's success ideals.

It is time to free yourself from the pressure of others' expectations of you.

Releasing yourself from the fear of others' opinions is an act of bravery that leads to your success in every area of life. Think about what you want your life to look like tomorrow, next month, next year, even five years from now—and plan accordingly.

ORGANIZE YOUR THOUGHTS AND PLAN YOUR FREEDOM

The planning and organizing phase of starting your very own business isn't just about putting certain goals and objectives on paper; it's not just about scheduling your day and coming up with a to-do list.

Planning also involves the mental preparation to work through all the emotions, temptations, and sometimes even logical reasons to quit!

Everyone knows for a fact that every now and then we face challenges such as busy schedules, family issues, work stress, and relationship problems. All are almost guaranteed in one form or another as part of your life at some point while you are working toward your goals. So be ready. When obstacles or difficulties pop up, remember that you knew they were coming, and you are ready and willing to keep working toward your goals, no matter what.

Releasing yourself from the fear of others' opinions is an act of bravery.

PLAN TO PERSIST

Always choose to make the right but sometimes difficult choices. If you want to succeed in your business, do the hard work up-front, make the tough decisions early on, then you can relax in your success later.

A tried, tested, true, and proven method to freeing yourself includes the following actions:

- Envision freedom.
- Plan and organize your methods and mentality.
- Take action every day.
- Make decisions without undue hesitation and thought.
- Celebrate successes along the way.
- Keep going even after success or failure.

When you decide to embark on a difficult journey—for example, start your business, lose weight, or any self-improvement effort—the world will throw its worst at you to challenge you, to see if you are serious or just talking like so many others. The world will check you, test you, and try you to see if your vision is real or just wishful thinking, once again.

Be ready to push through the initial resistance and bad fortune; they are only tests. After you pass through the fire, you will be stronger and the world will step aside as you walk on by toward achieving your desired goals.

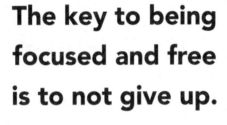

**The key to being
focused and free
is to not give up.**

IF AT FIRST YOU DON'T SUCCEED...

Sometimes your plans need to be revised. There may have been a critical detail you missed that sets you back and ruins the schedule you had established. When that happens, it's important to get back to the drawing board and begin writing a new set of plans.

There is no time to dwell on defeats or delays or even what might seem a colossal failure in the planning stage of your process. The achievement of your goals is founded on the strength and thoroughness of your planning, so don't hesitate! Go back and spend time rethinking what went wrong and why, then revise and implement the new plan. Repeat this process until you get it right—it's worth the effort.

DON'T RUN AWAY

Develop the habit of accepting life's difficulties, the unexpected drama and inconveniences, trials, hardships, poverty, hunger, etc. Face them all head-on. Build your work ethic through each of the setbacks and your character will become strong enough to withstand whatever challenges come your way.

If you feel the need to run and hide from all the opinions and advice from your loved ones, you may need to take some time alone to rebuild yourself—to regain the confidence and excitement you had when you first started this venture.

Take time to make yourself into the person you want to be. Doing what you need to do for yourself may mean escaping the influence and the noise of people around you who have told you all your life who you were supposed to be—who they wanted you to be. Taking this step will free you on so many levels.

HABIT ADJUSTMENTS

You will probably have to adjust your habits if you want to achieve your goals. For instance, if you typically stay up late at night watching TV shows or movies, playing video games, or surfing the Internet, you may have to give up those activities so you can get 7-8 hours of sleep then rise early to put in the necessary time to get your business off the ground.

Does your current daily routine prevent you from doing what you know you need to accomplish? If your bad habits are consistently more important than completing your to-do list, it's time to decide how much you *really want* what you *say* you want. Upon serious and honest self-reflection, if you decide that you *do* want to achieve your goals and free yourself from your current circumstances, then you must break every bad habit and replace each one with a good habit that will move you forward.

I know it's not that simple.

But it must become important to you to want to cut back and stay away from activities that are slowing you down and holding you

Decide how much you really want what you say you want.

back from becoming all you can be and having the successful business you know you could have.

Begin by prioritizing your good habits over your bad habits—every day, every night, every hour. Almost each moment everyone is faced with decisions, temptations, and distractions. In each case, we need to keep our goal of freedom above all and make the right decision.

CHOOSE YOUR RELATIONSHIPS CAREFULLY

Be careful when choosing friends and associates who will be close enough to influence you and your decisions. Plan to live your life according to your own values, ethics, and principles.

People may criticize you for your choices, but remember that people will criticize you for something no matter what. The more quickly you can move on from others' negative remarks, the better off you and your business will be.

Hang around people who motivate you to be better and to achieve more. Make friends with people who are making sound decisions in life. Learn from those who treat their customers with respect and courtesy and aim to give them the best experience possible, not only because it reflects well on their business, but also because it's the right thing to do.

Many of our habits are encouraged by the people closest to us.

AVOID COMPARISONS

There are millions of people with millions of goals, and not one was born with the exact same skillset or motives or levels of ambition as you. As you move through the steps and process of growing your independent business and reaching your personal goals, you will be tempted to compare yourself with others. This temptation has been exacerbated by the prevalence of social media, and many have fallen into the comparison trap, causing undue stress and even business failure.

Some people see carefully curated images of others' lives and careers as presented through various social media platforms and become jealous or feel badly about their own lives. They compare themselves to people who may or may not be portraying an honest view of themselves.

You are on your own journey and the only competition is within yourself. Be true to yourself and do what is right and you will always do your best work.

PLAN FOR QUALITY

When you make your business plans, err on the side of quality in your scheduling and your overall goals of customer service and delivery. Regardless of what you are providing, quality is king and queen. All it takes is a few negative reviews or disappointed customers to spread the word around and derail your efforts.

A high quality experience, on the other hand, will be prized and praised by your customers. So make sure to deliver on your promise with each business transaction. Deliver quality every time.

PRACTICE YOUR PITCH

After you decide what you are selling and how you will market your product and/or services, practice exuding an enthusiastic, pleasing personality that reveals your commitment and excitement about your business and product.

Not everyone was born with a God-given charismatic personality. But thankfully there are many ways to learn how to speak with confidence and a comfortable smile. It is worth your time to research the ways you can make or improve a first impression. The Internet is full of suggestions; choose only the tips that feel comfortable for you.

ORGANIZED DAYDREAMING

If you find yourself lost in thought with overlapping and overwhelming ideas, stop and grab a pen and paper or your phone, whatever, and write down a goal you would like to accomplish in the next hour. This is a little hack to reclaim your attention when it's been lost. Write down your vision. Write down your plans. Write down your strategy for pushing yourself through the down times and the disappointments of life.

Before you know it, you'll be looking at your goals and your plan with a focused optimism as you continue your work.

Organize your thoughts each morning and as often as you need to throughout the day. Remember that the secret to achieving is making a habit of controlling your attention.

FOCUS AND DIRECT YOUR MOTIVES

Do not look for validation from outside sources. You are your own best validation. You don't need anyone else's approval of yourself. It is easy to find ourselves working to make someone else happy, or working because we believe it is expected of us, or because we think someone will like us more if we achieve a certain status in society.

Make sure your motivation comes from within and plan and act accordingly. It will be much easier to stick to the plan if you believe in your reasons for doing it in the first place.

STRIVE FOR FREEDOM—AIM FOR ACTION

All this is part of the valuable habit of organizing and planning. You can see by now that much of this stage involves mental strategy. When you can organize, plan, and schedule your vision, it moves a little closer to reality; as you see the shape of your business, your goal becomes clearer.

As you dive into the process, it actually becomes fun and satisfying to prepare and plan. It feels good to be ready, to have goals, and to occupy your time with meaningful pursuits such as growing your business, strengthening your financial position, and helping others by being the best person you can be.

We must remember, too, that a follow-through action plan is crucial to finding the freedom we seek. It is easy to become trapped or stalled in the planning and preparing stages of your business. Progress can be delayed for weeks, months, or even years if we chase perfection within our plans before taking action.

QUESTIONS FOR REFLECTION

- What are two daily tasks you do not look forward to completing?
- Are there ways to avoid these daily tasks, or at least make them less daunting?
- Are you organized financially?
- Do you have "emergency" money set aside for an unexpected loss of income?
- Do you have money saved for vehicle/travel expenses?
- Are you saving and investing at least some of your money every time you get paid?
- What two activities do you plan for and look forward to? (Perhaps vacations, hobbies, etc.). What steps do you take in planning for those activities?
- What large goal can you begin planning for today?

Your goals are
too important to
leave them in the
dream phase.

Step 3

MAKE DAILY PROGRESS

"You must disobey the voice in your head that says,
I'm not ready yet."
—Marie Forleo, Author and Entrepreneur

There was a guy I used to work with at the machine shop—we called him The Professor because he wore an ivy cap (a newsboy hat) to work and was a teacher before he came to work as a machinist. He was an eccentric, intellectual type and tended to go deep into the technical aspects of everything he talked about. Anyway, I remember him talking to me about my dream of becoming a writer and he said something like, "Once you understand the ratio of effort to reward, you will realize your goal."

His comment stuck with me over the years, and now I see the truth of this statement. When I put forth a certain amount of effort, there comes with it a similar amount of reward. And now I notice the variance even on a daily level. For example, if my work is a weak, half-hearted effort, so is the reward. If I put in a great day of work, going above and beyond what I had planned, the reward is much greater.

The reward may not always be monetary. It might not always be a new client or a big sale, but you will notice it in your self-esteem, confidence, and demeanor. You will have a sense of satisfaction after having put in the conscious effort to continue your work or to overcome a temptation to procrastinate.

Another way to continue the momentum of your work is to push yourself to do a little more each time you think about stopping.

THE EXTRA MILE

Make it a habit to do more than you expect yourself or your followers to do. Followers in this case means your employees, direct reports, interns, assistants, and whoever else might be working with you in your business. Whatever you expect them to do and whatever you expect them to be at work, in terms of ethics especially, you must exhibit the same behavior. The bottom line: you are the role model.

Do more than you are expected to do as an employee—and do more than others expect you to do as a business owner.

If things have been slow lately, going above and beyond the usual can revitalize the productivity levels in your business. Sometimes there is a simple answer to rejuvenating yourself and your work life, such as *doing one more thing;* the proverbial "going the extra mile" can be the key to breaking through a plateau.

Even if business is going well, it can go even better when you make it a habit to apply this principle of going above and beyond what needs to be done for the day. Not only does going the extra mile reward you with increased productivity, it gives you something else worth even more—the gift of the present.

THE GIFT OF THE PRESENT

When you control your thoughts in the moment to the extent that you can make yourself work an extra 15-30 minutes, you are experiencing the power of living in the present moment. There was a minute when you were ready to call it quits and get something to eat, but you decided to do a little more—and in that moment you were living in the present moment, choosing to stay and work rather than quit and satisfy a momentary hunger pain.

Use the power of the present moment to take you deeper into accomplishing your goals.

Make it a habit to stay 100 percent present with whatever you are doing. Even if you are just cooking eggs for breakfast in the morning, practice the art of staying in the moment. Notice the details of the eggs frying—pay attention to only what you are doing right then. Focus.

As this practice becomes habitual, you will notice the increase in your productivity as well as in the quality of your work. Your level of

Use the power of living in the present moment to accomplish your goals.

creativity will increase from your heightened awareness of the inspiration and beauty around you. Problems will become less significant.

The present moment truly is a gift once you begin seeing and experiencing its benefits.

PROFESSIONAL AND PERSONAL

Another quick productivity hack is to sometimes mix your personal tasks with your professional work. Think about it; both are necessary for a smooth daily living routine. Yes, you still have to prioritize, but creating a to-do list that includes your work *and* personal tasks for the day will maximize your productivity and simplify your day-to-day life.

There is constant pressure to balance business and personal life, and often times that pressure is increased in our mind due to the way we too carefully separate the two aspects of our lives. Compartmentalization is necessary, but can be overdone. Relax into the realization that—in the big picture—both the personal and professional sides of our experience are fluid and not as separate as we might think they should be.

NO MORE LIVING FOR THE WEEKEND

> *"Some of ya'll are not where you want to be in life yet you party every weekend. What exactly are you celebrating?"*
>
> —T.I., Entrepreneur, Songwriter

What are we celebrating every weekend? The fact that we have two days off from our day job?

If at all possible, work on something you want to work on all week long rather than counting the days until Friday. Put time into your bigger goals instead of wasting time working for the weekend and then having a "good time" for a couple days before putting yourself back in the same unsatisfactory position on Monday.

TIME AND AGAIN

Since the industrial revolution, Americans have been increasingly motivated and socially programmed to obey the clock.

Few things stifle productivity more than the habit of constantly checking the clock, checking the status of your time. It is necessary at times, but constantly "keeping an eye on the time" can be a major distraction that prevents us from entering "flow states" and deeper levels of concentration. The realization of time stops momentum and creates stress.

Pause and imagine there are no more clocks, watches, calendars, or notions of time beyond day and night. Let your *focus* be more important than anything else—meaning, don't let outside influences interrupt what you are working on, if at all possible. Laser sharp, intentional concentration will take you far and fast on the journey of becoming focused and free. Therefore, prize the time you have to focus and you will soon reap the results of a productive day full of accomplishments.

Think of time in a different way to get more done. Don't limit yourself to the normal, socially accepted constructs when it comes to working toward your goals. How can you manipulate the idea of time to motivate yourself to do more and judge yourself less?

We can easily become servants of the clock, constantly waiting or looking ahead to the next conference call or appointment. Think of the moment you are in. Try to relegate time to this small window of the present. Being present shifts your focus away from the multiple other things you need to get done later and back to the task you are working on right now.

FOCUSED & FREE

TIME MANAGEMENT EXERCISE

Use your imagination to use measurements of time to your advantage. Use your newfound perspective of time to help manage your emotions and self-judgment. For example, instead of judging yourself for not getting enough done or worrying about the upcoming meeting, meditate on the idea that this is the only minute of the day you have.

The past minutes are gone, never to be experienced again, so stay in the present moment and prepare as best as you can for the next moment and the one after and so on. This exercise is really about breaking time down into smaller and smaller segments in order to focus the mind.

When you get worked up or stressed out due to the many tasks you have on your plate, recognize those feelings of stress and use them as triggers to calm yourself. Familiar emotions can be used as an impetus to acknowledge the absurdity of your worry. After all, anxious thoughts are not going to change anything. They will only make it more difficult to train your mind to pay attention to what *can* be done right now.

And by the way, if you work *better* under the stress of time and deadlines, use that characteristic to your advantage and create high intensity by manipulating your thoughts to imagine you have less time than you actually do.

If you can use your negative thoughts to jumpstart positive action or shift your thinking, you will make great progress toward becoming focused and free in your daily life.

92

USE NEGATIVE TRIGGERS

What I mean by negative trigger is any time you are tempted toward doing something that is a habit that takes your attention away from your goal, whether reaching for your phone unnecessarily or clicking on a browser to check the weather, read the news, or catch up on social media, pay attention and reroute your attention back to your goal. Every time you notice yourself actively seeking or engaging in distracting behavior, pause and reclaim your attention. This mental practice steers you back to your work.

Many of these exercises may appear as overly simplistic, but don't discount them before you try them. It is more useful to practice, practice, and practice these basic mental exercises than to seek out undiscovered methods of productivity that you hope will bring fast results.

I want to focus on the positive steps of establishing and operating a successful business, but the negative parts have to be addressed as well. Eventually, the positive parts of your efforts, business, and your life will so outweigh the negative to the extent that you barely notice your bad habits. They have become an afterthought and hopefully, no longer a habit at all.

A FREEDOM MINDSET

When you experience feelings of discontent, loneliness and anxiety, sit and meet with them.

The habitual desire for something different is one of the greatest tricks the mind plays—and marketing and advertising cultures encourage at every turn—making you think that there would be more pleasure, more comfort in doing something else, being somewhere else, or having something more.

Yes, there is a natural inclination to want more when it comes to our primitive, inherent desire for survival, but in today's world, it is a desire—fueled by constant advertising—that easily becomes habitual thinking.

Else, other, more , if only…

Feel the sensory pleasure of being alive without being distracted by the desire to do something else, and watch negative feelings subside over time.

Who you are is who you are, what you are is what you are, where you are is where you are. Accepting these basic facts—that's freedom. Freedom is in your mind. Knowing this allows you a clear starting point to envision your future, plan accordingly, make headway daily and act decisively.

Sometimes you have to work through some major mental battles and hang-ups. They amount to nothing more than distraction. This does not mean it is easy to shake them and get back to work. Sometimes it takes time and patience with yourself. You will get there if you don't give up.

MENTAL AWARENESS

Success comes down to mental fortitude. Fall into the habit of working within your headspace, your thoughts, to bring them under control, or at least direct them enough to take the tumbling mess of chaotic noise within your skull and turn it toward your work rather than something meaningless or detrimental.

Let yourself believe in the possibility of your "Acres of Diamonds," a wonderful and relevant story you will read in the Conclusion of this book.[1]

Sometimes it seems as if we're in a daze or a cloud. Try some hacks to shake yourself up and sharpen your mind. Things like exercise (walking), a dip in the pool, a cold shower, or even a nap. Shake yourself into a more focused mindset.

INTERMITTENT FASTING SHAKE-UP

I have found that there's a certain kind of crazy sharpness of mind when I fast. Denying myself food for a specific period of time can heighten my mental awareness to a point of chaos, and then I can watch myself mentally progress through the madness and eventually I'm at the center of it.

At the center of the storm, a great feeling of focus washes over me. My actions are precise, measured, and I no longer notice the hunger or anything much outside that tiny white, hot point of focus.

It's a concentration that feels almost drug-induced, yet I've only consumed water and maybe a little coffee or tea.

I believe that fasting is a fantastic, natural way to produce more, concentrate fully, and make progress on my goals. Make sure you discuss fasting with your doctor to make sure it is healthy for you personally.

DAILY MOTIVATION PROGRESS

As you knock daily tasks off your list, you are not only moving closer to your goals, you are also giving yourself additional motivation, little sparks of fire that will push you to continue onward.

This is your daily journey, and it lasts as long as you live.

You get to choose what road you want to travel on that leads to your desired destinations. Give yourself opportunities to experience the fullness of all your options by doing the work that leads to success. Give yourself the freedom to travel and experience all that life has to offer.

HABITS ESTABLISH YOUR DESTINY

There is much to read and learn about how we acquire habits, how we break old habits, and how we establish new ones. Learn what you can, what you need to when it comes to the habits in your life that you would like to replace or establish.

This is a highly personal endeavor.

Look at your life and understand that you can shape and change your life through the choices you make. Repeating those choices causes them to become habits.

Write a list of your current habits; then write a list of the new ones you would like to establish in your life. This exercise will give you an overview of what you do without thinking, and it gives you the opportunity to examine your actions from a different perspective.

- What do you want to change about your habitual actions?
- What makes you feel disappointed after you have done it?
- What do you get tired of doing?
- What makes you feel good about yourself when you finish?
- What habits are not on this list that you wish were on there?
- Spend time observing yourself throughout a typical day from when you wake up, at work, home, and during the evening.
- What are you easily distracted by or often mentally focused on?
- How often do you check your phone, email, social media?
- What do you look forward to doing each day?

There's so much to learn and gain from this simple exercise of paying attention to your habits, enough to acknowledge and cite them in writing.

THOUGHT HABITS

Our level of productivity is determined to a large extent by our habits of thinking.

I like to picture a circle that is made of our thoughts. For example, if we drift off to thoughts of fantasy (imagined riches, lack of problems) while we are overwhelmed by a stressful workload, we are much less likely to do the work needed to stop the feelings of being overwhelmed, which establish negative thought patterns recycling themselves to keep us in a certain state of undesirable feelings including stress, anxiety, and a sense of overwhelming despair.

If we default to thoughts of escape or pleasure when we are bored, we will make poor time-management decisions that leads us into situations that induced the feelings of boredom in the first place.

Our thought habits are cyclical and repetitive, producing results based on the wheel we allow to circle within. As much as possible, keep your thoughts within a wheel that produces the outcome you want for the long term rather than the immediate satisfaction of fleeting pleasures. Direct your thoughts into the wheel of productivity and experience a new kind of gratification.

Make it a habit to switch back and forth between productive tasks. For example, if you are trying to establish both the habit of writing and the habit of exercising—say, running for example—mix it up not only when you are unmotivated to do one or the other, but also when you are enjoying one or the other activity. Stop and work on the other habit.

Alternating between projects and initiatives works for several reasons:

- Switching between tasks enhances your ability to concentrate for longer periods of time.

- Switching between tasks lessens the amount of time you are susceptible to distraction.

- The fewer the distractions and the less time exposed to potential distractions, the better your chances at establishing your desired habits.

Remember, you can recognize unproductive habits by the amount of distracting thoughts that come with them.

THE POWER OF WORDS

It's been said that humans speak between 7,000 and 20,000 words every day. Let's say for the sake of discussion that it is 10,000. What could you do with 10,000 words that could not only improve your life, but also help others improve their lives?

How often do express words of complaint? How often do your words negatively describe yourself or your day?

We don't always feel positive, so it is fair to say that some of those 10,000 daily words will be negative; but if you make an effort to be more conscious about what you say, you can reduce the amount of

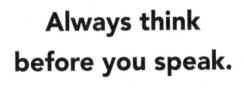

**Always think
before you speak.**

pessimistic or defeatist energy by thoughtfully and carefully choosing your words.

Intentionally choose words to bring you closer to your goals. Acknowledge the power of your words and make it a habit to put them to work for your benefit—always think before you speak.

NO PLACE FOR PERFECTION

There is no place for perfection in your journey to success. Allow your efforts to motivate you and move you forward. Avoid comparing your work to those who are further along in a field or industry similar to the one in which you are working. Stay as "original" as possible by working on your own objectives in your own way in your own timing.

Author Steven Pressfield writes in his book *The War of Art*:

> Resistance with a capital R, that force of self-sabotage, will try to stop you as a writer or an artist or anybody from achieving your best work, from following your calling, will try to distract you, undermine your self-confidence, make you procrastinate, make you quit, make you give into fear, or, on the other hand, make you such a perfectionist that you spend all day on one paragraph and you accomplish nothing. The concept of little successes, or of a routine, is to help you overcome that Resistance.[2]

Not comparing yourself with others minimizes feelings of inferiority or superiority. Keep making genuine efforts daily from the place of your truth, and eventually the results will bear out a story of success.

Your life well-lived is the goal. Your successful business will be part of that life. Make it a habit to avoid looking at results too frequently. Stay with the process and manage your expectations.

OVER AND OVER AGAIN

At times, life can take on a feeling of repetition. We can use that sense of repetition to our advantage by paying attention to patterns that work and patterns that don't. We can learn how to combat the wiles of our mind's weaknesses. Ultimately, it is about turning negative myths about ourselves into a positive truths to benefit ourselves. Daily we must recognize and fight against the dark side in us.

So when your mind starts nagging you about the pointlessness of repeatedly going into the office to earn money or work on your business in the face of continual failure and setbacks, understand that these moments of doubt are tests to determine just how much you really want what you say you want. No matter how long the test takes, use it as a lesson. It will provide you with tools to take you to the next level in your vision.

THE DAY WILL PASS

Make it a mental habit to slow down the pace of your energy. Some days we are nervous and scared, worried that we are not getting enough done. Mental games, social conditioning can contribute to these feelings of inadequate progress. Remember to use your mind, use your 10,000 spoken words per day to bring to life you thoughts and ideas that will propel you. Go forward, but don't rush.

The day will progress on its own. Work on mentally slowing time enough to accomplish the work required. All the words and stories continually passing through our mind—you can make a habit of weeding out the useless ones. You can choose which ones to keep and turn into something usable and which ones to throw away.

Think about it: Can you make it a habit to sit down and select your thoughts? Every time you go to work, can you choose what task you focus on and exclude all else until you are finished?

It is all about pointing your energy in a focused direction and keeping it there until the goal is reached.

ENERGY OUTPUT

Imagine putting your own energy out into the universe instead of only absorbing the energy of others.

When you are interested in being more productive, a good habit is to do one more thing on your list or as part of your current task before you go away from your work for any reason (assuming a non-emergency type of situation). To progress daily, adopt the habit of responding to one more email, loading one more skid, making one more phone call, taping one more video, packing one more box, writing one more paragraph, etc.

EMOTIONAL HABITS

To be successful in any endeavor, we must control our emotions. When emotions take over, logic and common sense usually fall by the wayside, which is not optimal when growing a business or in any work environment.

Establishing emotional habits begins with choosing what you think about. It's often said that life is 10 percent what happens and 90 percent how we react to what happens. And how we react is closely linked to how we think, or in this case, *what* we think.

For instance, fear can quickly control us in a variety of unhealthy ways—if we allow it. To help beat your fears, bring them out of the dark recesses of the mind and onto the examination table under a bright light. Make something out of them—a book, a movie, a painting. Release the horrible, anxious thoughts into something constructive, something healing.

Mental, emotional, physical, and spiritual habits are all tied together in making our success turn out the way we want it to. We have to react to the results of our choices with change or acceptance or maybe both. The key is to just keep moving, and the choppy waters will smooth out.

And of course, look around once in a while. Don't live your life entirely through your cell phone or television or your laptop. Sometimes it takes a little while to realize that you are enjoying yourself—and that maybe you have become your best friend and these moments of solitude bring great pleasure. Maybe there is no need to look for a source of more pleasure or greater pleasure. Let your thoughts flow freely.

SCHEDULE RELAXATION

When you are resting or doing something that may not be specifically furthering your goals, be okay with it as long as it is not something destructive. Because it is so easy to fall into the habit of self-criticism; taking the time to rest and relax and enjoy some downtime can go a long way in refreshing your mind and body and mental state.

No one is exceptionally productive every single day, so give yourself grace. There are days when every other obligation in your life—relationships, children, day job, health—will demand your attention—all of it—and before you know it, you are exhausted and ready to go to bed before getting the things done in your business or goal list that you wanted to accomplish. Maybe you can still take a few minutes and plan for the next day and that alone is considered progress. It is okay, you will make up the difference.

HABIT OF FINISHING

> *"Perhaps you are in the habit of leaving things unfinished, and the subconscious has gotten into the habit of not completing. As without, so within."*
>
> —Florence Scovel Shinn, Author and Illustrator

As discussed previously, our lives are full of habits—good and bad. Phone habits, Internet habits, reading habits, television habits, eating habits, the habit of setting unrealistic timelines and expectations, work habits, etc. There is also a habit of procrastinating; yet even within that habit there's a little voice inside telling us we need to *finish* what we begin.

Finish the day strong, the project, the workout, the conversation, the plan of execution, or even a list. The habit of finishing will bring you the most satisfaction of a job well done and increase the desire to replicate that feeling.

DO WHAT YOU DON'T WANT TO DO

When it comes to finishing tasks, a key component is the habit of doing the parts of the job that you don't like. It might be reviewing technical documents or a video call or an interview—whatever it is that you find unpleasant or you tend to procrastinate doing, those are the things you should do each day.

As a benefit, when you do things you *don't* enjoy, you will enjoy the things you *do* like doing even more.

HABIT OF ENCOURAGEMENT

Nothing motivates more than encouragement on a daily basis. At times, things like hunger, pain, or fear may be the impetus for action; but in the regular grind of life, encouragement is key. Encourage your spouse, children, colleagues, siblings, and friends. Most will receive it well, not all. It doesn't matter. Encouraging others helps you develop positive mental habits regardless of how people respond.

Control your mental habits and you can experience the closest thing to freedom this life can offer.

REWARD HABITS

Do you reward yourself when you complete a challenging task or is something you don't want to do?

Rewarding yourself reinforces positive behavior and prompts continued daily progress. In addition to the typical "rewards" of a dish of your favorite ice cream or an hour of gaming, give yourself the reward of working on your independent business or home-based business after you complete your day job tasks. Reward yourself with time doing the work you *want* to do after doing the work you *have* to do.

Working toward and reaching your goals is all about the reward of contentment, legacy, fulfillment, and your dreamed-of lifestyle.

Make it a habit to have an open mind that is susceptible to receiving new ideas; write them down. Don't allow yourself to be mentally paralyzed by all the options you have at a given moment. Choose the work and enjoy the work you choose.

Finish every task, and then reward yourself with a task you would rather do.

SOCIAL MEDIA

Use social media—don't let it use you.

Don't get sucked in to endless surfing or scrolling. Do what you intend to do on social media—create content, read a post, engage with other people, etc.—but then turn it off and move on to what else needs to be done. On Instagram, you can check your daily usage in the account features and see just how much time per day you spend on your feed. You may be very surprised!

Wasting hours on social media can be a costly trap in terms of lost business opportunities, damaged relationships, and/or loss of self-esteem. You can't retrieve the time you spend mindlessly consuming feeds on various social media platforms.

CRACK THE SHELL

Our habits can become our shell. If you want to shed your shell, the heavy mask of insecurities you have been carrying, work on stripping away habits that no longer serve you well—and maybe never did. Instead, focus more on establishing good habits that move your vision and work forward, and finishing projects.

Many of our habits are nothing more than defense mechanisms established when we were young children that we do not need anymore.

HABITS CREATE HABITS

Use the repetition of life to your advantage by creating productive habits to pass the time. Think about what you could accomplish if you used the moments you waste. Good habits and bad habits tend to pile up over time. They multiply, whether we like it or not.

For example, if you start a habit of exercising every day, you will probably start desiring to eat healthy foods to fuel your exercise. When you make a habit to finish projects, you find yourself wanting to start more projects to finish.

CREATE YOUR BACKSTORY

Who or what kind of person do you want to be known as? What parts of your story do you hope to have people remember?

It is our habits that finally define us. What you make of your habits is what you make of yourself. If you habitually make excuses like I used to do, you won't get much done toward creating a legacy or creating the story you want to be told about you.

> *"We are what we repeatedly do. Excellence, then, is not an act but a habit."*
>
> —Aristotle

THERE IS NO PERFECT PATH

The path you are on is the path you are on. Work from where you are and find a new path if necessary, but you must start from the place where you are. Try not to make excuses for yourself.

> *"Without continual growth and progress, such words as improvement, achievement, and success have no meaning."*
>
> —Benjamin Franklin, Inventor, Writer, Diplomat

Not starting your work is the only definite path to failure. As you begin, there will be obstacles and hardships, but the way through will always be there as long as you don't give up.

Everyone who is successful at doing what they want to be doing had to *start* somewhere. They may have been called "green," rookie, or newbie, but they *started*. Eventually, through continued work and persistence, they earned success.

Remember, it is easy to become trapped or stalled in the planning and preparing stages of your business. Progress can be delayed for weeks, months, or even years by chasing perfection within the plans. Be willing to take action.

This is especially true when you look at different ways and choices of doing things. This is why in the next chapter we will discuss the habit of arriving at decisions quickly.

QUESTIONS TO CONSIDER

- Are you satisfied with your current level of productivity?
- If not, in what areas do you want to be more productive?
- What are your main daily struggles?
- Are any of those struggles obstacles to your productivity?
- What can you do to eliminate or lessen the effects of those obstacles?
- How many hours per day are you willing to work, and for how many months or years?
- Do you often worry about what time it is and the next meeting, phone call, errand?
- What habits would you like to establish in your daily routine?
- In the evening, do you take time to reflect on your day and think about plans for the next day?
- Do you enjoy the feeling of finishing a task and crossing it off your list? How does it make you feel?

"Find certain things you know you
should do, don't like to do, or make
excuses to avoid, and then do them every
day or every other day, and then
it just becomes a habit."

—US Army General (Ret.) Stanley A. McChrystal

Step 4

DECIDE PROMPTLY

"More is lost by indecision than wrong decision.
Indecision is the thief of opportunity.
It will steal you blind."
—Marcus Tullius Cicero

As your business continues to grow and develop, you will be faced with more and more decisions to make. A key to success in this area is being wisely decisive.

EVALUATE, CONTEMPLATE, ACCELERATE

When it comes to making decisions, I use a three-step process:

1. Evaluate the choices.

2. Contemplate the results of each choice.

3. Accelerate into action your choice.

These three steps are self-explanatory in that we must clearly weigh the choices, then consider the consequences of each choice, and then make the decision and take the action necessary.

Making decisions is the way things get done. Nothing happens without someone first deciding to do something. For example, as I sit on the deck in my backyard writing this, my neighbor has decided to trim around all the places in his yard where the lawnmower can't reach. Maybe he will get his lawnmower out and cut the grass next. I can hardly wait to find out.

The point is that he made a decision within a span of time and followed through with it—hopefully to the task's completion. This is how lawn maintenance takes place. It begins with a decision made by the homeowner to act upon.

Of course, some decisions are easier to make than others. For example, you can decide not to get out of bed when the alarm goes off. Then you have another decision to make—whether to hit the snooze button or turn off the alarm entirely. Depending on your decision in those few groggy seconds, you will be given another set of choices as soon as you awaken.

Each day and subsequent measure of time—weeks, months, years—is filled with your decisions and the results, or consequences, of the choices you made. In part, the events of the day unfold according to your decisions. Some of the day unfolds due to chance, of course, but each choice you make puts you at the beginning of another potential outcome(s) that would not occur should you choose some other action.

For example, I have a decision to make right now. I can stop writing and sit here on the deck staring off into the distance and thinking on whatever random thoughts drift into my skull, many of which are useless. Or I can choose to keep writing my thoughts about decision-making, a topic I want to share with you from what I've learned.

When I make the latter choice, my decision puts that desire into the flow of life and I am given thoughts that are in line with that desire to grow and learn and share. All of which is part of personal growth and a good step toward a contented life void of all the what-ifs. Why? Because when you start making decisions more firmly, quickly, and precisely than you used to, you don't have as much time to dwell and wallow in doubt, ambiguity, or boredom.

DECISION-MAKING APPROACHES

There is the just-get-it-done approach to decision-making that can often clash with the get-it-done *right* approach.

If you struggle with making good decisions quickly, make it a habit to say something like, "I'll get back to you on this," or something to that effect. This response is especially appropriate if you have a habit of saying "Yes" too quickly (usually to make people happy), and then often have to go back and say "No" after evaluating the options and results of the decision.

Sometimes the get-it-done-*right* approach can lead to perfectionism, missed deadlines, and a consistent lack of completion and productivity. At the same time, the just-get-it-done mentality can lead to sloppiness and missed opportunities.

> *"In the words of the ancients, one should make his decision within the space of seven breaths. It is a matter of being determined and having the spirit to break through to the other side."*
>
> —Ghost Dog movie

Of course, not every decision should be made "within the space of seven breaths," but there is a piece of wisdom in this idea that can be used as a tool to become proficient in making decisions and sticking to them.

Practice for one day, making decisions within 10 seconds whenever possible. Try not to judge the outcome of those choices as good or bad, but instead remind yourself to focus on the decision itself.

Sometimes you will make the wrong decision. And sometimes you will make a decision that may not be clearly wrong, but another choice would have had better results. This, of course, comes with the knowledge you gain after the decision was made and the path became clearer.

COMMIT TO YOUR DECISION

> *"So often, we pretend we've made a decision, when what we've really done is signed up to try until it gets too uncomfortable."*
>
> —Jen Sincero, Author, Success Coach

Stick with your decision until you reasonably can't. By this I mean, once you've decided upon a course of action, stay the course until you are certain that it is wrong or until you succeed. Be quick to decide and slow to reverse the decision. There are times when you should reverse your decision, but those occasions should be few and far between. Napoleon Hill's book *Think and Grow Rich* says this:

> Analysis of several hundred people who had accumulated fortunes well beyond the million dollar mark, disclosed the fact that every one of them had the habit of reaching decisions promptly, and of changing these decisions slowly, if, and when they were changed. People who fail to accumulate money, without exception have the habit of reaching decisions, if at all, very slowly, and of changing these decisions quickly and often.[1]

If part of your goal of running your own business is to accumulate money, you would do well to heed the words of Hill and continue to develop the habit of reaching decisions quickly.

COST OF INDECISION

Think about how much time is lost going back and forth between options and not making a decision. Think of time we spent properly wording a text to a loved one that we are backing out of a commitment. Think of the guilt, the potential damage to relationships because we changed a decision at the last minute. Or we said yes when we should have said no.

> *"The most difficult thing is the decision to act, the rest is merely tenacity. The fears are paper tigers. You can do anything you decide to do. You can act to change and control your life; and the procedure, the process is its own reward."*
>
> —Amelia Earhart, Aviator

People are comfortable with a quick decision-maker. It often spares them the pressure to make the decisions for themselves when in a group setting and it makes them more apt to follow the one willing to make quick and firm decisions on matters.

There is a difference between quick and hasty. Quick decision-making is direct and according to a plan, while hasty decisions are made without thinking at all and often lead to more frequent mistakes and wrong decisions.

You will make mistakes regardless especially during your initial work to improve your decision-making skills, but the key is to "make mistakes of ambition, not of sloth," as Renaissance philosopher Niccolo Machiavelli put it.

TRUST YOUR ADVISORS

If you decide to seek advice when facing a business decision, look to those you respect and admire in a business sense. If it is a technology-related decision, ask for help from proven experts in technology. If a personal decision, ask someone who has been through a similar situation.

The point is, be careful with whom you discuss your important decisions. Think of seeking advice from a tactical standpoint. Some people may not be reliable when it comes to discussing personal or business matters.

ORGANIZE YOUR WORKSPACE

Prolific author and university cofounder Elmer Towns recommends organizing your workspace to minimize distractions and unnecessary actions to foster more prompt decision-making and better success in accomplishing your goals.

In his book *Homemade Rules for Success,* he shares the following tips:

1. Organize your desk to organize your work.

2. Stop handling paper twice.

3. Live by a list.

4. Let yesterday's list flow into today's list.[2]

Through simple, basic preparation you can reduce wasted time by quickly and wisely weighing several options—not *every* option, which leads to distraction. Defeat the procrastination habit by making a decision and then immediately, if possible, taking a course of action.

A simple, basic example follows: You have only 45 minutes to stop at the bank and get lunch before a meeting at work. You see a variety of grab-and-go restaurants and before you get overwhelmed with all the options, you make the wise decision to pull into the one closest to the bank. Therefore, you made a quick but logical decision that was the most time efficient.

Making quick decisions about small issues prepares you for making bigger decisions. If you make a wrong decision, don't feast on guilt. Learn from the mistake and move on.

Decide and act, decide
and act, because all the
while your thoughts
will arise and pass,
arise and pass.

PRACTICE

Use the mundane daily situations of your life to practice making prompt decisions. When ordering lunch and trying to decide between a sandwich and a pizza, don't ask for other people's opinions, just pick one—the world will not stop spinning if you take a bite and it isn't as tasty as you had hoped. Next time you'll choose the pizza!

When asked a yes or no question, answer yes or no to the best of your knowledge. Make sure you understand what is being asked before answering. Right now, we're talking about inconsequential issues that you can practice with being decisive. Of course, always use your best judgment.

We often do not realize how unsettled, ambiguous, and indecisive we are. In business, these traits can be seen as less than credible. Think about what changes you can make to be a more decisive person. When making daily small choices, be assertive and honest with yourself and others.

WHAT WILL THEY THINK?

There's no more certain way to waste valuable time than to consistently wonder what others think about your decisions. To be free of the fear of other people's perceptions, you must choose to make decisions and put yourself out there. Taking risks is part of a full life.

To be vulnerable yet in control of your life is being all you can be, fully alive.

Facing reality head-on you know that people are going to be critical—either to your face or behind your back, and it doesn't much matter. Older folks will tell you that when they reached a certain age, it became clear to them that most people didn't care as much about them as they thought. We overestimate the amount of thought others give our actions and decisions. It is best to make the best decision you can and move on—regardless of others' opinions.

Better decision-making skills open more doors and that means more different choices are coming your way and new decisions will need to be made. New decisions, different decisions but also familiar decisions in different contexts. Also, those new decisions and choices mean new and varied opportunities for experience and potential growth.

CONSCIOUS DECISIONS

Have you ever thought about how many of your decisions are not made with your conscious mind?

For example, just before I wrote that sentence, I stopped writing, reached over to the coffee table, picked up my glass of water, and took a drink. I don't remember thinking about doing that even for a second. Or how about the way you're fidgeting with something right now as you read this. Are you tapping your fingers, wiggling your foot, or playing with a pen or with your hair?

We do many things every day that we don't consciously decide to do, which makes some people question the validity of our freedom to choose certain actions. Some say that involuntary actions can be explained biologically and neurologically—and even our conscious decisions can be explained by our nature and the nurture of our upbringing, claiming that all decisions are essentially predetermined, and to an extent fixed and predictable by our inherent "programming."

I think in day-to-day life, it is practical to accept that we have free will to make decisions. We cannot see time and space from a fourth dimension that tells us how our life will play out, so we must live and be present in our daily existence as it is, making decisions when the need arises.

For some people, there is a benefit of comfort to be had in seeing everything as predetermined, in the sense that "all is as it will be." In other words, they think that no amount of worry or anxious thoughts will change anything. It is already decided. However, this can be a horrific viewpoint for other people who need to be in control.

MINDFULLY NUMB—REMOVE EMOTION

Multibillionaire Warren Buffett has said, "You will continue to suffer if you have an emotional reaction to everything that is said to you. True power is sitting back and observing things with logic. True power is restraint. If words control you, that means everyone else can control you. Breathe and allow things to pass."

Making decisions can be challenging. You have to weigh the pros and cons, and this careful evaluation can be exhausting, nerve-wracking, and even scary. Avoid these feelings as much as possible by removing emotions attached to the possible results. In other words, if you are angry or resentful, you are more likely to make a poor decision resulting in disaster.

THE COURAGE TO MAKE A DECISION

Consider these thoughts from Napoleon Hill:

> The value of decisions depends on the courage required to render them. The great decisions, which served as the foundation of civilization, were reached by assuming great risks which often meant the chance of death.
>
> Lincoln's decision to issue his famous Proclamation of Emancipation, which gave freedom to the enslaved people of America, was rendered with full understanding that his act would turn thousands of friends and political supporters against him.
>
> Socrates' decision to drink the cup of poison, rather than compromise in his personal belief, was a decision of courage. It turned time ahead a thousand years, and gave to people then unborn the right to freedom of thought and of speech.[3]

Rarely do we realize the impact our decisions—especially the courageous ones—can have on not only us, but our loved ones in future days and years. Think about what decisions you have made that you are proud to have had the courage to make. Are you sticking by those decisions today?

Arriving at wise decisions quickly is a habit fostered by envisioning your goals and working toward them habitually. The desire that you feel when you imagine your success is the fire that will fuel your work to attain your goals. Allow yourself to feel the burning desire and immediately proceed with whatever it takes to move ahead. Strike while the iron is hot, as they say.

Making decisions promptly frees up time rather than wasting it while floundering around in indecision. You will notice the wonderful feeling of freedom when you habitually make decisions quickly.

CHARACTER BUILDER

Decision-making will turn you into a more honest character. You will become more truthful and up-front about what you like and don't like, about what you want and don't want. At times, especially if you are a people-pleaser—aka approval junkie—by nature and/or nurture, this newfound honesty will feel uncomfortable, and people may bristle at your candor. It's okay. You will get used to it and so will others.

It will be refreshing to be open and honest with people—and that's what happens when you quickly yet wisely respond. Being candid—not hurtful or judgmental—is good for others too as they will know better who you are and will act accordingly. Make decisions, stick with them, and don't pretend that you have a choice in the matter. There are times you should reverse your decision, of course, but these times should be few and far between.

When you choose a path, dream about what the imagined life could be, take action, and make daily decisions that move you closer to your goal. Keeping your destination in mind means you have less time to be tempted to veer off course. You are determined to make choices that align with your purpose. That means ignoring the options that will slow you down and choosing the options that propel you along the right path in the right direction.

When you are determined and your vision is clear:

- You will avoid negative-energy people.

- You won't carouse all night and miss important meetings in the morning.

- You won't abuse your body and mind in ways that negatively affect your health.

- Your whole mindset shifts to an efficient progression of success throughout each day.

- Each day takes you nearer to living your dream life.

Decision making is not relegated to your business such as deciding which products to buy and sell, at what prices, which marketing strategies to follow, and so on. It is also about deciding to be optimistic even after accidentally sleeping in. It is deciding to be positive even when you are not looking forward to the tasks that need to be completed that day. It means deciding to react with kindness and understanding even when someone chooses to be rude to you.

Decide to minimize distractions.

Decide to exercise for at least 15 minutes today.

Decide to do one thing today that you don't want to that will bring you closer to your goal.

Decide to keep working when you feel like stopping.

Decide to eat a piece of fruit when you feel like eating a candy bar.

All these daily choices can be made more consciously for great improvements to your daily life.

QUESTIONS TO CONSIDER

- Do you consider yourself an indecisive or decisive person?
- In what areas of your life do you wish to make decisions more quickly?
- How much time do you waste in indecision every day? Every hour?
- How would your personal life improve if you were more decisive?
- In what ways would your business and/or work life improve if you were more decisive?
- Think of several people who are decisive. What other characteristics do they have?

"*Every day you are faced with decisions. Where you end up in this world is up to you. You have the opportunity to shape your legacy. Your legacy is based on your vision, the way you think, and the decisions you make. Most times there is so much more that is available to us, but we do not realize it. It is only available if we make the conscious choice to be that person or pursue that endeavor. It is your decision.*"

—Sam Silverstein,
Author of *Making Accountable Decisions*

Step 5

CELEBRATE VICTORIES

The more you praise and celebrate your life,
the more there is in life to celebrate.
—Oprah Winfrey

CELEBRATE YOURSELF

What have you accomplished today?

What did you get done that you can be proud of, happy about, or simply relieved to have it off your list?

Maybe you're not as far along as you hoped you would be by now. But! You are further than if you had never started. The same amount of time would have passed and you likely would be exactly where you were when you started. So give yourself credit for at least moving ahead.

When you celebrate reaching goals and objectives whether big or small, you will discover that it motivates you to keep going for more.

Each morning decide what tasks you want to complete that day and also think about a reward or celebration to mark your accomplishment. Your reward or celebration may be taking your partner out to dinner. Or if a larger celebration is warranted, you could put your other goals on hold for a bit with a vacation from work—be it an afternoon of golf or a week at the beach.

CELEBRATE WITH OTHERS

No one gets to the top alone. I have no doubt that long the way others have helped you finish a project, brainstorm a problem's solution, meet a deadline, etc. Think about the past few months at work, home, and your relationships in general. Who has helped you? Now think about ways you can thank them with a small but sincere celebration.

Helping others ultimately results in a sense of satisfaction that goes a long way in developing a healthy self-esteem. Putting other people first makes them feel important and encourages them. In turn, celebrating every encounter with others will invigorate your creative inspiration.

Thank the people who have helped you achieve your goals and have supported you along the way from the dreaming phase on to the completion, the realization of that dream-turned-reality. Make an effort to listen to others' dreams and goals and be open to supporting them as well.

As discussed previously and as you well know, there are distractions bombarding us at all times, so it is critical that we learn to focus

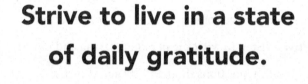

Strive to live in a state of daily gratitude.

not only on our business goals, of course, but also the individuals we need to help us reach our goals.

A few common-sense reminders:

- Always greet people with a smile and a handshake (or fist/elbow bump).
- Avoid being rude by reading or texting on your phone while in a conversation with someone face-to-face.
- Give your full attention to the person in front of you.
- Being polite and attentive makes people feel special and they will definitely remember the way you treat them.
- Never gossip or speak unkindly about others—whether the others are present or absent from the conversation.
- Actively listen to what the person is saying and don't interrupt.
- Respond to questions thoughtfully and directly.
- Offer genuine compliments, not insincere flattery or platitudes.

Leaving an impression of friendly professionalism will go far in generating a network of people who can benefit each other.

GRATITUDE FOR VICTORIES

It's a good day when you get ideas down on paper, scheduled, organized, and ready for action—but before you do this, take a moment or two to be thankful for the opportunity to grow your business, to

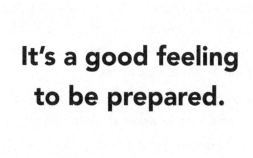

It's a good feeling
to be prepared.

work on your body, for your family, or to achieve your financial and organizational goals.

Begin from this mindset and it will be easier to weather the setbacks that will inevitably come your way during the day. Make it a habit to adopt a positive attitude each morning and you will have more than enough energy to carry you through the day.

Of course, everyone has some bad-mood, ungrateful days. When you recognize this is a reality of life, it gives you more power to change your attitude as much as possible. The more often you can change your attitude—not dwell on negative thoughts—the more it will become habitual to mentally control your attitude. You will automatically take control of feelings that may include resentment, stress, and overall poor thoughts—turning them into positive thoughts of gratitude, refreshment, and high hopes.

When you are prepared for an onslaught of inevitable negative thoughts, you don't have to worry about the consequences of succumbing to them. Why? Because you are ready. You turn them away as quickly as they come. Preparation is key.

BECOME A PREPPER

In 2020 when the coronavirus started spreading around the world, a wide variety of human reactions ensued. Governments issued warnings, then mandates, and people were panic-buying groceries and other supplies, afraid of what might happen and envisioning worst-case scenarios.

Some people, often called "preppers," were already prepared. They had plenty of food and supplies stored away and could stay safely inside their homes for long periods of time without exposing themselves to the virus. They knew how good it felt to be ready, to be prepared. No doubt they celebrated more than once with a full stock of cleaning supplies, tissues, and toilet paper.

Those who organize and plan and invest financially will enjoy celebrating if the economy takes a downturn. When you work on strengthening your finances and saving money, you will be prepared if you happen to lose your source of income for a while.

Likewise, work on strengthening your body so you are in shape should you have to do physical activity for long periods of time to survive or make it to the next step in your journey.

After working on these areas of your life, celebrate and enjoy the boost of feel-good energy from being ready. Time spent in preparing yourself and your family for difficult circumstances is never wasted. Knowing you are prepared frees your mind space for additional creative and/or productive activities.

> *It is necessary then to cultivate the habit of being grateful for every good thing that comes to you, and to give thanks continuously.*
>
> —Wallace D. Wattles, Author

It is almost impossible to have a negative attitude when you practice being grateful each day. In fact, it is a tremendous mood booster just to think of and name what you are thankful for at any given time. The habit of gratefulness will quickly lift you out of a funk and is an important tool to have on your journey toward making daily progress in achieving your larger goals.

Be grateful for the opportunity to better yourself. Give thanks for the mental capacity to dream of new ideas and goals. What else can you be thankful for right now in this moment? Write a few and then celebrate each one:

_____

_____

_____

_____

_____

_____

_____

_____

_____

_____

_____

_____

_____

> *"Make an affirmation immediately upon waking. For example, 'Thy will be done this day. Today is a day of completion. I give thanks for this perfect day. Miracle shall follow miracle, and wonders shall never cease.' Make this a habit, and one will see wonders and miracles come into his life."*
>
> —Florence Scovel Shinn

TRY, TRY AGAIN

Increasing the number of opportunities you try actually improves your chances of success. The more times you try, the better your chances of succeeding. The same is true of what are called failures— the more you fail, the more opportunities you have to evaluate why you failed and to make improvements for the next time you try.

> *"Celebrate your success and find humor in your failures."*
>
> —Sam Walton, Walmart Founder

Success in life is a "numbers game." Increase your chances of success by increasing the number and frequency of your efforts daily, weekly, and monthly.

> *"Work like hell. I mean you have to put in 80- to 100 hour weeks every week. This improves the odds of success. If other people are putting in 40-hour workweeks and you are putting in 100-hour workweeks, then even if you're doing the same thing, you know that you will achieve in four months what it takes them a year to achieve."*
>
> —Elon Musk

I realize not everyone is wired like Elon Musk or Steve Jobs or other notorious world-changing workaholics blessed with brilliant minds and a relentless drive, but most of us could be so much more if we did the things we already know we could do to improve.

Examine your efforts. Evaluate how much time you have actually spent working toward that goal you so desperately want to accomplish. Test your motives. Are they lacking sincerity? Are they shallow?

> *"Celebrate what you've accomplished, but raise the bar a little higher each time you succeed."*
>
> —Mia Hamm, Olympic Soccer Gold Medalist

You may not have your business up off the ground and making money because you are putting in less hours a day than necessary. You might be blaming external factors like day job work-related stress or family responsibilities for what is truly an internal lack of commitment, the weakness of your resolve. Assess yourself, take an honest look inside to see if the lack of success is actually linked to your lack of desire.

PLAN YOUR NEXT GOAL'S VICTORY CELEBRATION

Part of becoming focused and free is achieving one of your goals so that you are free to begin achieving the next one. It is a simple thought process, yet an important one.

When you complete step one, you begin step two. It is a concept that is taught into us from a young age. We have to relearn it and benefit from it to move to the next level.

It's a great habit to make time every day, or at least every week, to write down one new thing you learned. What did you learn today? Yesterday? The past week? Write down one thing you've learned each day. The lesson learned could have been the result of a negative experience, a positive conversation, or a seemingly trivial phone call.

Intentionally recognizing lessons learned and writing them down will expose what is and isn't working regarding a variety of issues: business, relationships, communication, etc. Doing this type of introspective evaluation, along with acknowledging your successes, provides insights needed to continue toward victory.

Find a way to share with others what you have learned to help them in their journey as well. It's repetitive but critical to your continued growth and independence.

ENJOY A LUNCH BREAK

Today's world is a whirlwind of constant connectedness with a focus on increasing the speed of productivity. It is easy to fall into the habit of eating lunch in the car, on the go, or sitting at your desk and wolfing down a sandwich. To refocus, reset, and refresh yourself for the afternoon's work, try adopting the habit of sitting down to eat, away from your desk, with a colleague or friend and having a nice chat—not necessarily about work.

Greek philosopher and sage Epicurus reportedly said, "We should look for someone to eat and drink with before looking for something to eat and drink." In today's fast-paced world, this is excellent advice and a great habit to help you expand your work and pleasure networks. Many connections, new ideas, and helpful times of relaxation and laughter happen over a meal.

Celebrating victories can be as simple as pausing to enjoy lunch and discuss life with another human being. When was the last time you paused for lunch with a someone?

And by the way, while at lunch, take the bold step to turn off your phone. The world will not come to an end if you don't answer a text or voice mail message. We have been programmed to respond to every text, and to be fearful about missing any world, national, local, and even Facebook "news." How legitimate is a majority of what we would miss during a lunch hour?

I have a cell phone *and* a landline, a relic of the past. People are surprised to see it and many make comments about this phone. It intrigues young visitors and evokes memories in older folk of times when life was simpler. When there was less pressure to communicate 24-7. Times when people communicated face-to-face or through letters and long-distance phone calls. During those times people wrote eloquent words in letters that would take a week or two or a month to arrive in the receiver's outdoor mail box. And long-distant calls cost money, so each brief conversation was valued and important. Times when generations of families lived in the same hometown area and their entertainment was high school football games and church suppers.

Today, many text messages, emails, Instagram and Facebook postings are full of inconsequential ramblings of little use. I urge you to choose your words, written and spoken, as if they were to be read by the person you admire most. That way, your communication with others will always be meaningful and significant.

FREEDOM FROM IRRELEVANT BELIEFS

One of the most satisfying reasons to celebrate is when you experience the victory of letting go of a belief that has no relevance. It could be a lie or a concept that no longer serves you or your goals. Overcoming a misconception can be a monumental victory for you, especially if it has kept you in some sort of bondage.

A lifetime of fallacies or unhealthy traditions from our parents, siblings, religious leaders, television, teachers, and/or friends are absorbed into our minds from the time we are old enough to understand and process them. Freeing yourself from corrupt, negative, or false beliefs is a huge step toward more success and a life of liberty. Some of these ideas and beliefs from your past you may choose to keep, but give yourself the permission to dismiss the ones that no longer serve you.

This freedom of mind will allow you to look at life, decisions, and business from new perspectives and you will find yourself one step closer to freeing yourself to be the person you want to be.

CELEBRATING TOO OFTEN, TOO EARLY

Some people party every weekend or every chance they get, which prevents them from making any headway toward reaching their goals. If that is you, it may be time to stop and think about what you are celebrating. Are you partying just because you don't have to work your day job for two days? Really?

It's okay to rest and recuperate, but some are celebrating achievements they haven't made yet. Or they are still celebrating an achievement from weeks or months ago. Over-celebrating can keep you stuck in the dream phase of your journey.

> "Remember to celebrate milestones as you prepare for the road ahead.
>
> —Nelson Mandela

You have to sacrifice some of those fun weekends to find success. Try not to lose sight of your vision just because your friends, family, and coworkers are content to live the status quo. They might want you to join them, but remember to focus on your goals and you will celebrate real victories.

Times of remembrance and reflection of wins and lessons learned and growth experienced along the way are all motivational tools necessary for the next leg of your exciting life's journey. But when the celebration itself becomes the point of the party, it is time to reevaluate and get back on the right path.

Keep working hard toward reaching your goals and living your dreams—then celebrate!

Step 6

KEEP GOING

"One of the most common causes of failure is the habit of quitting when one is overtaken by temporary defeat."
—Napoleon Hill

Step Six is to keep going—going directly to your destiny of being free to be yourself.

ALL WISH, NO WORK

We all know people who frequently come up with great ideas and big wishes and ideals for their lives, but never change their way of living or thinking to make those ideas, wishes, and ideals become realities.

Break the habit of
wishing for success
without taking
any action.

We have to break the habit of wishing for success without taking any action to attain it. The distraction of fantasy and "wishful" thinking is a costly mistake that gets us nowhere.

Once you remove the tendency to wish instead of work, you are on your way to establishing the effective habits that will bring you the realization of your independent business or improved self.

Dreaming of success and fantasizing about being a certain kind of person—someone to admire—is easy and can distract us from actually *doing* the things we don't want to do, but know we should be doing. While at your day job, think of how quickly and easily you can be led into wishful thinking of being somewhere else or doing something else for a living.

The following are three ways to combat this problem of wishful thinking getting in the way of meaningful action. To make daily progress and keep going:

1. ***Develop the skill of concentration.*** Playing games such as chess, solving crossword puzzles, and piecing together jigsaw puzzles can help with training your brain to concentrate. Also contributing to concentration improvement is a good night's sleep, exercise, nature walks, meditation, music, healthy diet, and a moderate amount of caffeine.[1]

2. ***Practice focus sprints.*** Focus on a task for an increment of time, say 5 minutes to start, then increase to 10 minutes, 15, etc. Using the power of focus will increase your productivity. Period. If you increase your productivity, you increase your value and your ability to reach your goals.

3. ***Train your mind to embrace the process over the result.***
   Every time you find yourself fantasizing about what it will
   be like when you have accomplished your goal, go and DO
   something—even if it is a small thing—that brings you closer to
   accomplishing it. By doing this over and over again, you train
   your mind to respond to that kind of thinking with ACTION.

Making headway or being productive is not only about getting
things done, sometimes it is only about getting *one* thing done; or
more importantly, maintaining the perspective of confidence in
yourself that allows you to believe you *will* get everything done that
needs to be done.

Even if you like what you are doing, there will be some aspect or
some circumstance in your personal life that you don't enjoy and
find ways to procrastinate. This is why you must develop the mental strength, fortitude, and self-assurance that you *will* complete the
task, even if tomorrow.

POSITIVE SELF-TALK

Bombard yourself with positive talk, regardless of your mistakes.
Healthy self-esteem is the goal—not arrogance or hubris. A good
dose of pats on the back and "good for me" expressions will lift your
confidence, spirit, and frame of mind. Appreciate yourself as you
would appreciate a good friend. In fact, talking to yourself kindly
and compassionately will improve your outlook and may even
relieve physical issues.

**Overthinking
is the enemy.**

On the other hand, when we struggle with guilt and shame, we often imagine our words and behavior as more embarrassing or negative than it really is. We latch on to anything that can make us feel badly, or especially guilty, and it becomes a negative habit we must overcome. It is easy to get pulled into our thoughts and allow them to spiral into all manner of useless—many times negative—patterns, images, memories, and regrets. When this happens, it is time to *think* and *do* something positive. Overthinking is the enemy.

Negative thinking is one of the fastest ways to derail your efforts—it can and must be overcome. The second you start doubting yourself and criticizing your work, remember you are good enough and that criticizing yourself is a waste of time. Get something done and move one!

FEELING GOOD AT THE END OF THE DAY

Positive feelings come from putting in a good day of work. When you don't accomplish much, how do you feel at the end of your day? I feel stressed out, maybe some guilt, and a little bit unsure of myself. These negative feelings aren't always fairly attributed and there's no sense in dwelling on them. The point is, when you're productive, you feel good. Period. So aim to feel good as often as possible by focusing on the prize of a job well done.

How often do our minds use old memories to serve as explanations and justifications for harboring resentments? Move on. No time or mental peace should be wasted on foolish thoughts about past

No negative thoughts today. Stay busy, stay calm, and master your emotions.

injustices and hurt feelings. If the wound was meant to be healed it will be healed. Otherwise, let time heal as it may.

If you are a sensitive person, you will have to make a conscious effort to change your thought patterns when negative thoughts arise. While difficult, it can be done successfully, and each time it gets a bit easier. You have to begin by knowing yourself and understanding your strengths as well as your vulnerabilities due to your personality.

KNOW YOUR WEAKNESSES

What are your common distractions and in what circumstances do you find yourself wasting time? Notice the triggers and react accordingly to refocus. Do you spend a lot of time fantasizing, daydreaming?

Is it working on the computer with easy access to the Internet? Is it texting on your phone or scrolling through endless social media feeds looking for something that will captivate your attention for a while?

When we behave like this, we are stuck in a cycle of procrastination by distraction—and we waste a lot of precious time that could have been put to good use. Write down a few things that you know are obstacles to your focus or your achievement. They could even be good things in and of themselves, but they are attended to or used at the wrong time, which causes you to become inattentive on your goals. Or the things you write down might be activities that you are drawn to that simply waste time.

Whatever these objects, activities, or forms of distractions are, you must recognize your inclination toward them and find a solution to eliminate, work around them, or and minimizing the influence they have on you.

It would be beneficial to investigate the reasons you are drawn to these distractions in the first place, but the main point is to write them down in front of you so you can see each one, think about it, figure out what to do about it, then *do it*.

MINIMIZE DISTRACTIONS

A big part of why some prison inmates can master massive amounts of tedious work—for example, write long books, build extremely fit bodies, craft ingenious tools or weapons—is because they are stripped of the profuse distractions of the outside world. That is not to say they can't find useless ways to spend their time, but the lack of options is a key dynamic of their situation, which contrasts greatly with the average "free" person's comfortable, busy, distracting, option-laden circumstances.

A lot of "getting stuff done" comes down to keeping yourself in the chair or focused on whatever task you are working on now. How can we keep focused with so many distractions surrounding us? That is the million dollar question.

To begin, stop asking others what they think of what you are doing. Just keep working instead. Don't quit. You may only be a few hours away from your 10,000-hour breakthrough. Author Malcolm

Gladwell theorized that it takes 10,000 hours to become an expert in your field or industry. The preciseness of this theory can be argued, but the point is that you will experience a certain breakthrough in your work of choice—provided you continue to put in enough time to achieve your goals and get better at what you do.

Ultimately, the way to minimize distraction and prolong your focus and concentration will come down to your ability to filter outside input and then fall in love with your resolve and with the results!

PERSEVERANCE

Perseverance is more valuable than talent when it comes to your business success. Again:

There will be many moments when it seems like it is not working out or you feel as though you made the wrong move and you want to quit and take a safer route in life. If you can get into the habit of not giving in to your emotions, you will climb up out of the low spots, overcome momentary failures, and build the character it takes to be persistent each day.

With this habit comes success. It might not come as quickly as you hoped or even planned, but it will come as long as you keep working toward your vision.

> *"A little more persistence, a little more effort, and what seemed hopeless failure may turn to glorious success."*
>
> —Elbert Hubbard

To keep going is not only important when adversity comes and you are tempted to quit, it is also important when you experience triumph and are tempted to rest in your success for too long. When you establish the habit of continual forward progress, you will be prepared to succeed again and again.

During crises and difficult times in your life, it can be tempting to cheat on working toward your goals and neglect your daily ambitions to improve. It's easy to write off bad food choices, lack of exercise, and forego your work to the ideal that you are merely "surviving" and that alone is success. Surviving may be success, but don't fool yourself into thinking you can't do better when you can.

For example, during the worldwide coronavirus quarantine, did you use the time to read and exercise to improve your mind and body? Or did you spend the time watching television and eating too much out of boredom or stress?

Get used to temporary discomfort—and you will enjoy the comfort even more. You will notice a deeper sense of awareness of the contrast between comfort and discomfort when you experience both. Reject the mundane when possible; find meaning in every

Perseverance is more
valuable than talent
when it comes to your
business success.

circumstance; search for it; suffer through it to find the positive, interesting, and useful aspect of an uncomfortable period of time.

DON'T GIVE UP

Don't give up until you're done with the project, finished with the book, completed the task, opened the doors to your business, etc. Keep pushing forward through the haze, the maze of your distracting thoughts and desires.

Push through the pain and exercise after you blew your diet, drank too much, and want nothing more than to fall down onto your bed and go to sleep. Look at your business plan, get something done off your list when you are tired and want to take a nap.

When you are feeling down, depressed, or stressed, turn to your business, your personal goals, your side hustle, and accomplish one thing. Anything. Just one. It's simple and it's doable and you will be surprised how much better you feel afterward.

Don't stop. All you have to do is get started on one little thing, one step, and then before you know it, you'll be into it and making progress toward your dreams.

A lot of what kills people's efforts is the lie that once they fail, mess up, and/or neglect their work for a week, a month, or whatever, that means they're past the point of becoming successful. People start labeling themselves as losers, quitters, or lazy at this point. They start telling themselves they aren't cut out for the business they want to run or start. They tell themselves that they aren't the type of person who can live a fitness lifestyle or curb their diet.

Don't let this be true of you!

The labels we give ourselves and the stories we tell ourselves are fiction stories, not true stories or labels that reflect our authentic selves. Change the narrative—write a true-life story of the come-back kid. Get up and get to work even if it feels like you're starting from square one. There's no better place to start.

Never tell yourself you are not what you want to be as a result of personal failure.

If you realize *through hard work over time* that the business you chose is not sustainable, or the lifestyle you aspire to is too far out of your character, that's different. Through introspection and efforts put forth in a certain direction, you may find out you need to change your goals, but don't change them or give up on them just because you fail on a personal level such as being too shy or too young/old or from the wrong neighborhood.

SELF-DOUBT OVERLOAD

For me, as soon as I decide on a topic to write about, I'm filled with self-doubt. *Maybe the topic is a poor one, too dull, I think. Maybe no one is interested, maybe I don't have enough material on that topic for a book…*maybe this, maybe that.

Can you relate to these feelings of inadequacy and fear?

Self-doubt always slows progress. Keep moving forward despite your fears and doubts. Perseverance distinguishes those who accomplish their goals and those who don't.

> *"The genius thing that we did was we didn't give up."*
>
> —Jay-Z, Songwriter and Record Executive

Imagine the worst-case scenario happening and decide within yourself that you are strong enough to keep going even after the disaster. Another benefit of this mental exercise is being able to prevent the worst-case scenario from happening, just by having thought through it ahead of time.

But what if?

What if you lost it all—all the work you put in for hours, days, even months—by some stroke of bad luck or your own mistake, you lost it. Gone. What do you do?

Discipline yourself to keep the work going especially when you are feeling down and out; let go of your desire to quit and take the easy way out. There is no easy way, there's only one way and that is to keep working. The only way out is through.

Remember that you had to start once before, you can do it again. You are being given a chance to redo what you should have done differently before.

There is no easy way, there's only one way and that is to keep working. The only way out is through.

REJECT THE LABELS

You will not have a proper perspective of yourself if you constantly look at other people to gain their respect and approval. This is a bad habit that slows you down. When you get rid of that mindset, the world opens up and you can see so much more detail. And as a pleasant side effect, you open yourself up to the world, finally accepting your flaws and come across as more authentic than ever before.

Be open to experiences as they happen. Here and now, present to the second.

Overthinking is useless regret. No overthinking and no anticipating unnecessarily. Present minded and moving forward. Let it go. You are yourself in forward motion, no emotion, nothing stopping, nothing stalling, everything ready to be born, reborn.

Be strong, this is the version of you that you have been waiting for, looking for, working toward. Everyone is flawed, so love yourself and love everyone else. Serve others, be a better person for other people. Make things right the best you can and help other people make the world better.

What are you waiting for?

Whatever your vision of success is, whatever your calling, the longer you spend time working toward that end, the more time will pass that you might typically fill with negative habits, thinking, and obsessing over normal and common human fears.

Rather, busy yourself with focusing on your plans and dreams and freedom.

Give yourself a reason to make each choice rather than drift along and face regret.

Do not get caught looking for pleasure or focusing on results. Stay deep in the process, it's the process we crave.

> "I maintained a small constellation of side jobs for seven years before I was confident enough—emotionally or financially—to rely solely on my business for full-time income. Throughout those years, I seized every moneymaking opportunity I could to pay the bills. I cleaned toilets. Worked thousands of shifts as a bartender and waitress. My dream of running my own business, on my own terms, doing exactly the kind of work that I do now, was so important that I was willing to do whatever it too, for as long as it took, to see it through."
>
> —Marie Forleo, *Everything is Figureoutable*

"It's hard to keep going when it seems like you're not getting anywhere, but you'll never succeed if you stop. Those of us with a dream that seems so far from being realized must remember that the road is long, but only those who stay on the path will reach their destination."

—Thomas Mann

Conclusion

YOUR ACRES OF DIAMONDS

I want to leave you with a story.

One of the most valuable habits you can establish in your quest for success is to learn how to find the resources, tools, and personal talents available to you right now—not only to finish the immediate job, but also to give yourself the best perspective possible. A major element of controlling your perspective is looking within yourself for answers that you try to find from others.

Develop the instinct to look within yourself, recognize and focus on what you can do *right now* that will eventually become your acres of diamonds that lead you to individual and financial freedom.

The *Acres of Diamonds story* was originally written or told by Russell Conwell and I share a key excerpt here that beautifully illustrates the visual imagery behind the idea.

When going down the Tigris and Euphrates rivers many years ago with a party of English travelers, I found myself under the direction of an old Arab guide whom we hired up at Bagdad, and I have often thought how that guide resembled our barbers in certain mental characteristics. He thought that it was not only his duty to guide us down those rivers, and do what he was paid for doing, but also to entertain us with stories curious and weird, ancient and modern, strange and familiar. Many of them I have forgotten, and I am glad I have, but there is one I shall never forget.

The old guide was leading my camel by its halter along the banks of those ancient rivers, and he told me story after story until I grew weary of his story-telling and ceased to listen. I have never been irritated with that guide when he lost his temper as I ceased listening. But I remember that he took off his Turkish cap and swung it in a circle to get my attention. I could see it through the corner of my eye, but I was determined not to look straight at him for fear he would tell another story. But although I am not a woman, I did finally look, and as soon as I did he went right into another story.

Said he, "I will tell you a story now which I reserve for my particular friends." When he emphasized the words "particular friends," I listened, and I have ever been glad I did. I really feel devoutly thankful, that there are 1,674 young men who have been carried through college by this lecture who are also glad that I did listen.

The old guide told me that there once lived not far from the River Indus an ancient Persian by the name of Ali Hafed. He said that Ali Hafed owned a very large farm, that he had orchards, grain-fields, and gardens; that he had money at interest, and was a wealthy and contented man. He was content because he was wealthy, and wealthy because he was content.

One day there visited that old Persian farmer one of these ancient Buddhist priests, one of the wise men of the East. He sat down by the fire and told the old farmer how this world of ours was made. He said that this world was once a mere bank of fog, and that the Almighty thrust His finger into this bank of fog, and began slowly to move His finger around, increasing the speed until at last He whirled this bank of fog into a solid ball of fire. Then it went rolling through the universe, burning its way through other banks of fog, and condensed the moisture without, until it fell in floods of rain upon its hot surface, and cooled the outward crust. Then the internal fires bursting outward through the crust threw up the mountains and hills, the valleys, the plains and prairies of this wonderful world of ours. If this internal molten mass came bursting out and cooled very quickly it became granite; less quickly copper, less quickly silver, less quickly gold, and, after gold, diamonds were made.

Said the old priest, "A diamond is a congealed drop of sunlight." Now that is literally scientifically true, that a diamond is an actual deposit of carbon from the sun.

The old priest told Ali Hafed that if he had one diamond the size of his thumb he could purchase the county, and if he had a mine of diamonds he could place his children upon thrones through the influence of their great wealth.

Ali Hafed heard all about diamonds, how much they were worth, and went to his bed that night a poor man. He had not lost anything, **but he was poor because he was discontented, and discontented because he feared he was poor.** He said, "I want a mine of diamonds," and he lay awake all night.

Early in the morning he sought out the priest. I know by experience that a priest is very cross when awakened early in the morning, and when he shook that old priest out of his dreams, Ali Hafed said to him:

"Will you tell me where I can find diamonds?"

"Diamonds! What do you want with diamonds?"

"Why, I wish to be immensely rich."

"Well, then, go along and find them. That is all you have to do; go and find them, and then you have them."

"But I don't know where to go."

"Well, if you will find a river that runs through white sands, between high mountains, in those white sands you will always find diamonds."

"I don't believe there is any such river."

"Oh yes, there are plenty of them. All you have to do is to go and find them, and then you have them."

YOUR ACRES OF DIAMONDS

Said Ali Hafed, "I will go."

So he sold his farm, collected his money, left his family in charge of a neighbor, and away he went in search of diamonds. He began his search, very properly to my mind, at the Mountains of the Moon. Afterward he came around into Palestine, then wandered on into Europe, and at last when his money was all spent and he was in rags, wretchedness, and poverty, he stood on the shore of that bay at Barcelona, in Spain, when a great tidal wave came rolling in between the pillars of Hercules, and the poor, afflicted, suffering, dying man could not resist the awful temptation to cast himself into that incoming tide, and he sank beneath its foaming crest, never to rise in this life again.

When that old guide had told me that awfully sad story he stopped the camel I was riding on and went back to fix the baggage that was coming off another camel, and I had an opportunity to muse over his story while he was gone.

I remember saying to myself, "Why did he reserve that story for his 'particular friends'?" There seemed to be no beginning, no middle, no end, nothing to it. That was the first story I had ever heard told in my life, and would be the first one I ever read, in which the hero was killed in the first chapter. I had but one chapter of that story, and the hero was dead.

When the guide came back and took up the halter of my camel, he went right ahead with the story, into the second chapter, just as though there had been no break.

The man who purchased Ali Hafed's farm one day led his camel into the garden to drink, and as that camel put its nose into the shallow water of that garden brook, Ali Hafed's successor noticed a curious flash of light from the white sands of the stream. He pulled out a black stone having an eye of light reflecting all the hues of the rainbow. He took the pebble into the house and put it on the mantel which covers the central fires, and forgot all about it.

A few days later this same old priest came in to visit Ali Hafed's successor, and the moment he opened that drawing-room door he saw that flash of light on the mantel, and he rushed up to it, and shouted: "Here is a diamond! Has Ali Hafed returned?"

"Oh no, Ali Hafed has not returned, and that is not a diamond. That is nothing but a stone we found right out here in our own garden."

"But," said the priest, "I tell you I know a diamond when I see it. I know positively that is a diamond."

Then together they rushed out into that old garden and stirred up the white sands with their fingers, and lo! there came up other more beautiful and valuable gems than the first.

"Thus," said the guide to me, and, friends, it is historically true, "was discovered the diamond-mine of Golconda, the most magnificent diamond-mine in all the history of mankind, excelling the Kimberly itself.

The Kohinoor, and the Orloff of the crown jewels of England and Russia, the largest on earth, came from that mine."

When that old Arab guide told me the second chapter of his story, he then took off his Turkish cap and swung it around in the air again to get my attention to the moral. Those Arab guides have morals to their stories, although they are not always moral. As he swung his hat, he said to me, "Had Ali Hafed remained at home and dug in his own cellar, or underneath his own wheat-fields, or in his own garden, instead of wretchedness, starvation, and death by suicide in a strange land, he would have had 'acres of diamonds.' For every acre of that old farm, yes, every shovelful, afterward revealed gems which since have decorated the crowns of monarchs."

When he had added the moral to his story I saw why he reserved it for "his particular friends." But I did not tell him I could see it. It was that mean old Arab's way of going around a thing like a lawyer, to say indirectly what he did not dare say directly, that "in his private opinion there was a certain young man then traveling down the Tigris River that might better be at home in America."[1]

This story illustrates a powerful truth that I believe can be applicable to each person. What is right in front of you that you could use to achieve your dreams and goals? What if we looked inside ourselves each day to mine the diamonds within our hearts and minds?

What if we believed that we were living with the power—the diamonds—to free us and change our lives beginning today? What if we reprogramed ourselves to believe that?

The next time you find yourself blaming your bad habits, your work-related stress, or family responsibilities for your lack of being who you want to be, make yourself take a long look inside.

You may find that the obstacles, the sticking points, the things that hold you back aren't external; you might find your failures come from within.

Are they not the failure of commitment, the weakness of your desire, the vagueness of your goals, or the lack of persistence and a willingness to give into distraction?

All you need is within, but you have to believe it and take the time to look inside and look at your life and your abilities exactly as they are to find your own acres of diamonds. Don't become complacent and satisfied with a mediocre experience of life.

Go for it and don't settle for the glory-day stories of "if only." Live your dreams now.

DON'T GET STUCK ON "IF ONLY"

We sometimes focus too much on the material world. We focus too closely on the injustices of our own little circle of being, all the ways things could be better—rarely do we consider how they could be worse—and all the things that we could do *if only...*

If only what?

- If only I had made different decisions
- If only my parents had raised my differently
- If only I had been born to different parents
- If only I hadn't been born into a family of this religion or into a home with no religion
- If only I hadn't met this person
- If only I had not married
- If only I had married
- If only I had kids
- If only I had no kids
- If only I did not live so far away
- If only I had not bought that house, invested that money, or spent that money foolishly
- If only my personality was more like his, or my upbringing more like hers...

If only, if only, if only—and meanwhile the earth just sits here in the galaxy, slowly turning, unconcerned, unmoved about any of it. It just sits there like it has for millions of years and will for millions more.

Live your life forward. There's no turning back.

> *"While people brood, time skips ahead without looking back."*
>
> —Alan Lightman, Physicist, Entrepreneur, Professor

Free yourself to create the business of your dreams. Free yourself to create the healthy lifestyle that you imagine. Free yourself to be the spouse, parent, friend others need. Follow the steps and learn the lessons our parents tried to teach us. Look at people who are where you want to be and imitate their best qualities.

Focus on the habits that will eventually allow you to be free: mentally, physically, financially, and spiritually.

The "new you" will not regret it.

LIFE LESSONS FROM ELBERT HUBBARD

The mind is a dual affair—objective and subjective. The objective mind sees all, hears all, reasons things out. The subjective mind stores up and only gives out when the objective mind sleeps. And as few men ever cultivate the absorbed, reflective or semi-trance state, where the objective mind rests, they never really call on their subconscious treasury for its stores. They are always self-conscious. Do not fear being misunderstood; and never waste a moment thinking about your enemies. Try to fix firmly in your own mind what you would like to do, and then without violence of direction you will move straight to the goal.

Thanks for taking the time to read this book. Would you please take a few more minutes to leave a brief review on the online bookseller of your choice? Thank you.

NOTES

STEP 2

1. Jason Murdock, Humans Have More than 6,000 Thoughts per Day, Psychologists Discover," *Newsweek,* July 15, 2020;

2. Napoleon Hill, *Think and Grow Rich Today* (Shippensburg, PA: Sound Wisdom, 2021).

3. Zig Ziglar-Nightingale Conant, *Sell Your Way to the Top* (Shippensburg, PA: Sound Wisdom, 2021).

4. Jim Stovall, *The Art of Entrepreneurship* (Shippensburg, PA: Sound Wisdom, 2021).

5. Contributor, "From Mailroom to Boardroom: 10 Modern-Day Execs Who Started at the Bottom," *YoungUpStarts.com;* June 5,

2012; https://www.youngupstarts.com/2012/06/05/from
-mailroom-to-boardroom-10-modern-day-execs-who-started
-at-the-bottom/; accessed July 27, 2021.

6. https://www.fundable.com/learn/startup-stories/spanx; and
https://www.britannica.com/biography/Sara-Blakely; accessed
July 27, 2021.

7. Rose Leadem, "9 Inspiring Quotes From Self-Made Billionaire
and Spanx Founder Sara Blakely," *Entrepreneur.com*, September
12, 2018; https://www.entrepreneur.com/slideshow/319539;
accessed July 27, 2021 and https://www.azquotes.com/
author/1493-Sara_Blakely?p=2; accessed August 1, 2021.

STEP 3

1. Reference to *Acres of Diamonds* by Russell H. Conwell, founder
of Temple University in Philadelphia, PA, who in essence reveals
that each person has wealth beyond measure close at hand. He
wrote that Americans have every opportunity to make more of
themselves within their own environment, with their own skills,
and with their own energy, and with their own friends.

2. Steven Pressfield, *The War of Art* (New York: Warner Books, 2003).

STEP 4

1. Napoleon Hill, *Think and Grow Rich* (Shippensburg, PA: Sound Wisdom, 2017).

2. Dr. Elmer Towns, *Home-Made Rules for Success: Thinking Your Way to the Top* (Shippensburg, PA: Destiny Image Publishers, 2016), 31-34.

3. Hill, *Think and Grow Rich*.

STEP 5

1. Crystal Raypole, "12 Tips to Improve Your Concentration," *Healthline*, September 3, 2019; https://www.healthline.com/health/mental-health/how-to-improve-concentration#takeaway; accessed July 31, 2021.

CONCLUSION

1. Public Domain

ACKNOWLEDGMENTS

Thank you to Dave Wildasin for encouraging me to keep writing, finishing, and publishing. Heather for squashing my self-doubt and excuses at every turn and holding me accountable. Riley and Kaden for keeping me grounded. Nathan for the hours of conversations about books and ideas and life. Angela R. Shears for helping shape my jumbled mess of thoughts. Eileen Rockwell for yet another beautiful cover design. Jeff Hall for an awesome page design.

ABOUT THE AUTHOR

JOHN MARTIN shares years of experience and insights to help people analyze their mindset through introspection so they can eliminate whatever is suppressing their potential—and release whatever is begging to emerge. His goal is to motivate and free people to take action and persevere regardless of their current situation.

In addition to *Focused and Free*, John has also received acclaim for his other personal development books:

- Empower Yourself: 7 Steps to Personal Success
- Increase Your Personal Productivity: Your Guide to Intentional Living & Doing More of What You Enjoy
- Choose Your Perspective: 7 Tips for High Performance through Intentional Thinking

www.soundwisdom.com